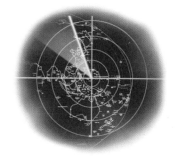

This edition © 2003 Grandreams Books Limited

Written by Peter Eldin
Edited by Joanna Davies and Nichola Tyrrell
Illustrated by Q2A Design Studio

Published by
Grandreams Books Limited
4 North Parade, Bath BA1 1LF, UK

Printed in China

THE
GREAT BIG
BOOK OF
FACTS

▼

Fantastic Facts and Questions and Answers
fully illustrated in colour

THE
GREAT BIG
BOOK OF
FACTS

500
FantasticFacts

Contents

Mythical Beasts

In the myths, legends and folklore of old there are many strange creatures with unusual powers. None of them really existed, but in days gone by many people believed them to be real.

The phoenix was a mythical bird of Egypt. According to legend, it lived for 500 years, then burnt itself to death on a large fire. After death, it was reborn and rose from the ashes. It was also thought the ashes could bring the dead back to life.

Around the world stories have been written about dragons. Most depicted these mythical fire-breathing creatures as monsters. Some dragons, however, such as those of Chinese mythology, were considered quite friendly.

The most famous statue of a sphinx lies near the Pyramids of Giza, Egypt. Originally built to guard the Khafre pyramid, it was also woshipped as a god. Its nose, sadly, was destroyed in later years by soldiers using it for target practice.

In Roman and Greek mythology, one look from the eyes of a basilisk was said to be enough to kill someone. Its breath was deadly too. Considered the king of the serpents, the basilisk was also called a cockatrice, for it was hatched by a serpent from a cock's egg.

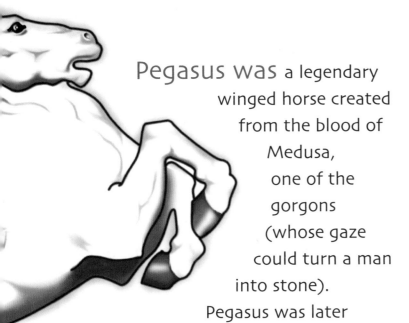

Pegasus was a legendary winged horse created from the blood of Medusa, one of the gorgons (whose gaze could turn a man into stone). Pegasus was later transformed into a constellation when it flew up into the sky.

One of the few beautiful creatures of fable was the unicorn, which resembled a horse but bore a single long horn in the centre of its forehead. Its body was white, its head was red and it had blue eyes. The horn was believed to have magical properties. Those who drank from it were thought to be protected from poisoning, stomach ailments and epilepsy. Many people thought the unicorn could tell if a liquid was poison just by dipping its horn into it. A unicorn is depicted on one side of the British royal coat of arms; opposite the unicorn is a lion.

Centaurs, according to Greek legend, were a race of creatures who were half man and half horse. They lived on the plains of Thessaly in central Greece and were well known for their lawless and riotous temperament.

In Greek mythology, the chimera was a female fire-eating monster that was part lion, part goat and part serpent. She was slain by a young warrior called Bellerophon, aided by Pegasus, the famous winged horse.

The Greek sphinx was said to be the daughter of the chimera. She had wings, a woman's head, the body of a lion and a serpent's tail. At the town of Thebes, so legend had it, the sphinx would ask travellers riddles. If they answered incorrectly, she would kill them.

Monsters of the World

Monsters?

Ridiculous, they do not exist! Well, that is what many people believe. Yet there seems to be a lot of evidence to suggest that some of the incredible stories of fantastic creatures could have an element of truth.

Some people believe there are several creatures in Loch Ness. They suspect that they are the descendants of prehistoric creatures. Thousands of years ago the loch was connected to the sea. Over time, the level of the land around the loch rose and the creatures were trapped.

Is there a monster in Scotland's Loch Ness? The insurance company Lloyds of London seems to think so. Lloyds refused to insure a Scottish whisky company against paying a reward of £1,000,000 for the capture of 'Nessie'. The insurers believe there is ample proof that something does live in the loch.

Lake Storsjon in Sweden is said to be the home of a monster that has a small head on a three metre-long (9.8 ft) neck. Its body is reportedly grey covered with black spots.

The first recorded sighting of the monster in Scotland's Loch Ness was made by St Columba over 1500 years ago. Over the years several photographs of the Loch Ness monster have been published but almost all have been proved to be fake.

In 1924 a prospector, Albert Ostmann, claimed that he had been kidnapped by a sasquatch from his camp in the middle of the night and taken to the creature's home. He was held captive for six days before managing to escape and tell his story to the world.

Nessie is not alone in the world. Other Scottish lochs also have their monsters, which the Scots call 'water kelpies'. Loch Morar boasts a monster the size of an elephant, called Morag. Despite the fact that a glimpse of Morag is said to kill the observer, there have been many reported sightings.

On the snow-covered slopes of the Caucasus Mountains in southwest Russia, there lives a monster that is rather like the Abominable Snowman. Known as the Almas, it measures about two metres (6.5 ft) in height, is covered with black hair and has a broad flat nose. Sightings of the creature have been reported for over 2000 years but no-one knows for certain if it really exists.

The Canadian cousin of the loch monsters Nessie and Morag is the ogopogo. Reportedly spotted in Lake Okagagan, British Columbia, this serpent-like creature is thought to measure from 10 - 20 metres (32 - 65 ft) long. First sightings of the ogopogo were recorded in 1872.

Monsters of all types have long hounded seafarers. Largest of these denizens of the deep is the awesome Kraken. The Kraken has been described as a giant octopus, squid, sea serpent and whale! It was first reported at the beginning of the 18th century off the coast of Norway. According to superstition, the Kraken is so big that many sailors have mistaken it for an island and actually landed on it and drowned when the creature suddenly submerged!

On 8th November 1951 the British mountaineer and explorer, Eric Shipton, took photographs of footprints in the snows of the Himalayas. Many people believe the footprints were those of the legendary Yeti, also known as the abominable snowman.

The Yeti, or abominable Snowman, is a giant legendary creature thought to live in the Himalayan Mountains.

Fantastic Fish

Most fish will die if removed from water. Yet the Lung fish of Africa, Australia and South America often spends long periods out of water. Its body is adapted to breathe air and during periods of drought the lung fish digs a hole in the mud. Slime from its body forms a protective cocoon until the water returns.

The bluefish hunts in schools that may extend up to 7 kilometres (4 miles) in length, This vicious predator has earned the nickname 'sea piranha'.

The red-bellied piranha is one of more than a dozen species of piranha found in northern South America. A school of these ferocious creatures can tear a victim to pieces in seconds.

Of all the sea's creatures, the most magnificent is surely the manta ray. There are stories of mantas eating people but, in fact, they are quite harmless, preferring to feed on plankton (minute organisms that drift in the ocean). Often manta rays will leap out of the water up to a height of four metres (13 ft) to rid themselves of small parasites. When they fall back into the water, the resounding crash can be heard for miles.

The sunfish is sometimes called the head fish, because it does not appear to have a body. It can grow up to two metres (6.5 ft) in length and yet its backbone measures only two centimetres (0.78 in) long.

The coelacanth is the only surviving species of a prehistoric group of fish, the Crossopterygii, from which some scientists suspect the first vertebrates evolved.

As its name suggests, the electric ray can give a powerful electric shock. Its shoulder muscles are capable of emitting up to 200 volts, which would knock a man over should he accidentally tread on one.

The African cat-fish lives in a topsy turvy world - it spends most of its life upside down! No other fish adopts this position, unless it is sick or dead. For camouflage, most fish are dark on top with a light underside. Because it is usually upside down, the African cat-fish has reversed this colouring with a silvery back and a dark belly. Its Latin name 'batensoda' means 'black belly'.

The electric cat-fish, found in African rivers, can grow up to a metre in length and is capable of producing a nasty electric shock. The ancient Egyptians believed the electric cat-fish to have magical powers and pictures of them have been found on the walls of tombs.

Cat-fish get their name from the long, whisker-like barbels around their mouths. These barbels are very sensitive feelers that allow the fish to live in deep water or be nocturnal because they can feel their way around in the dark.

When threatened with danger the Puffer fish inflates itself, with water or air, up to three times its normal size! This defence strategy may scare off predators or suggest the fish is too big to be eaten. And yet the Puffer fish does get eaten - by humans. It is a great delicacy in Japan, where it is called 'fugu'. The liver of the Puffer fish contains a powerful poison, so Japanese chefs have to attend a special fugu cookery school to learn how to prepare it properly. In spite of these precautions, many people in Japan still die from fugu poisoning. Also called blowfish or swellfish, puffers are mostly found near coral reefs in tropical waters.

The porcupine fish, like the puffer fish, inflates itself when under threat and it is covered with hundreds of prickly spines. Its second line of defence is its sharp teeth. When swallowed by a larger fish the porcupine fish simply eats through the flesh of its enemy!

Creatures in Disguise

Many animals are not equipped to fight their enemies and therefore need to hide from them. Some creatures dig holes in the ground to hide. Others are rather clever, for they disguise themselves. They transform themselves either to mimic other creatures, or to match their background.

Ladybirds produce a liquid so unpleasant that birds will not eat them. Several other insects, which are probably quite tasty to the birds, have developed the same markings as ladybirds as a form of protection.

The ptarmigan, a type of bird, changes its colour to match the seasons. In summer its feathers are speckled to match the earth and grasses where it lives. But when winter comes the bird loses its speckled feathers and grows white ones, making the ptarmigan more difficult to spot in the snow.

Some fruit flies flap their wings to mimic the territorial display of their main enemy, the jumping spider. This fools the spider into thinking that the fly is actually one of its own!

The caterpillar of the king page butterfly has an unusual disguise for its protection: it looks like a bird dropping!

The chameleon can change colour very quickly. When on the ground its body is green with yellow spots and it has bright yellow legs. When it is in the trees turns completely green to blend in with its surroundings.

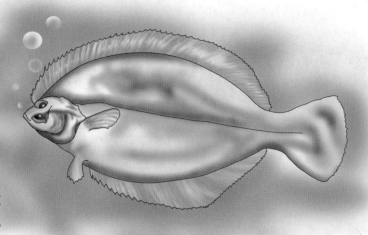

Like some birds a number of fish can change colour as well. Flatfish, such as plaice and flounder, can match their colours to those of the sea bed.

The buff-tip moth has wings that are the same colour as the tree branches on which it lives. To make itself even more difficult to see, the buff-tip wraps its wings around its body, so it looks like a piece of broken twig.

A lot of creatures look like others as a form of protection. The monarch butterfly of North America is ignored by birds because it tastes horrible. The viceroy butterfly has copied the markings of the monarch to make birds think that it, too, is unpleasant.

The stick insect is so called because it looks like a stick. It is the same colour as a stick and when very still on a branch it is almost impossible to spot.

Many insects resemble leaves. They have the same colouring and often the same shape as the leaves on which they live. The dead-leaf butterfly of Malaya is aptly named – when it folds its wings, so only the underside is visible, it looks just like a dead leaf!

The hover fly has the same markings as a wasp. The wasp can sting a predator, so if the hover fly looks like a wasp, its enemies will avoid it.

Another creature that uses seaweed as a disguise is the leafy sea dragon, a type of seahorse. It is actually shaped like seaweed but also hangs onto a piece of seaweed to make the disguise more believable. To hide itself from enemies the decorator crab covers itself with bits of seaweed or moss.

Mysteries of Migration

Many birds move to warmer parts of the world during the winter months. This annual journey is called migration. It is a subject that has intrigued mankind since the beginning of time.

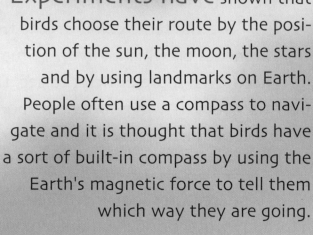

Experiments have shown that birds choose their route by the position of the sun, the moon, the stars and by using landmarks on Earth. People often use a compass to navigate and it is thought that birds have a sort of built-in compass by using the Earth's magnetic force to tell them which way they are going.

The snow bunting nests in many places in the Arctic Circle but it spends the winter in Britain.

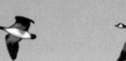

Not all birds undertake such long journeys. Many sea birds just move inland a little during the winter months and many birds do not migrate at all.

By examining the weight, food intake and flying ability of the ruby-throated hummingbird, scientists have shown that the bird could not possibly store enough energy to fly from Florida to Central and South America. But the hummingbird does it just the same!

Some migrations involve incredibly long journeys. The longest is that of the Arctic tern, which travels from the Arctic Circle to Antarctica - an annual return trip of more than 17,500 kilometres (11,000 miles). The common tern makes a comparatively short journey each year - from North America to Africa!

One of the mysteries of migration is how birds manage to find their way. They appear to follow coastlines that no longer exist; it is likely that they use the sun and the stars to guide them.

The kittiwake breeds in Northern Europe but moves to Southern Europe for the winter.

Hooded cranes breed in Alaska, the Aleutian Islands and Siberia. They fly to Japan in the autumn and return northwards the following spring.

About one third of the birds which breed in the British Isles spend the winter in Africa.

Tristan da Cunha is a tiny island in the South Atlantic which is almost 3000 kilometres (1864 miles) from the nearest land. Each year great shearwaters fly to this tiny speck in the ocean to lay their eggs.

AFRICA

ATLANTIC

OCEAN

Ascension Island

St Helena

Tristan da Cunha

Amazing Nests

There are many different types of birds' nests. Some birds do not build nests at all, but lay their eggs on the bare earth. Others build nests that are so unusual they are simply amazing.

The female hornbill

nests in a hole in a tree while she waits for her eggs to hatch. The entrance is plastered up with mud and twigs by the male. Just a small hole is left open and the male feeds his mate through the hole while she incubates the eggs. When the eggs have hatched, the female breaks out of her prison to help the male gather food for the chicks.

The tailor bird

of India simply does a bit of sewing to make its nest! Firstly, the bird pokes holes through some leaves. Then, using its beak as a sewing needle, it threads vines through holes to sew the leaves together.

Weaver birds

take great care to weave their beautiful nests, which hang from tree branches.

After laying an egg, the albatross scratches up the earth around it, forming a protective ring.

As its name suggests, the burrowing owl has its nest in a burrow in the ground. Sometimes the owl will dig the burrow itself but often it simply takes over the burrow of some small animal. The actual nest, which can be several metres underground, is lined with grass and other materials for comfort.

The social weavers of South Africa build a large, umbrella-like structure in trees. They then build individual nests inside this protective covering. There can be as many as several hundred birds living under one main roof!

The brush turkey of Australia builds an enormous mound, some five metres (16.4 ft) high, for its nest. The mound, on which the bird lays its eggs, covers a pile of rotting vegetation. The heat produced by the decaying plant material keeps the eggs warm. Each day the male bird tests the temperature of the nest and if it becomes too warm he will make ventilation holes to cool it down.

Flamingos build their nests by forming a mound of mud in the lakes in which they breed. The mound is then hollowed out to store the eggs. The nests are high enough so they cannot become flooded and are built closely together in a colony.

In the lakes high up in the Andes Mountains of South America, there is very little vegetation for the horned coot to build its nest. The bird solves this problem by building a tower of stones in a lake, and then putting its nest on top of the tower. The tower itself, consisting of hundreds of stones, can measure up to four metres (13 ft) in circumference at the base, and up to one metre (some three ft) in height.

Flightless Birds

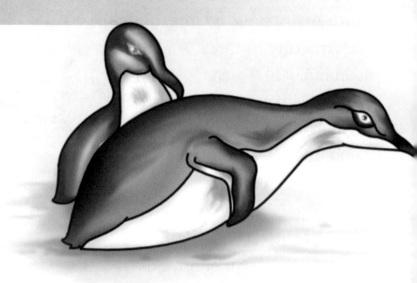

Most birds are wonderfully constructed flying machines, yet there are quite a few, such as the penguin species, that cannot fly. Many flightless birds are found on islands where they have no natural enemies, so there is no need for them to fly.

Once the mother emperor has returned from feeding, she will take over caring for her chick. Then it's Dad's turn to eat!

Living along the southern coast of Australia is the fairy, or little blue, penguin. It measures some 30 centimetres (12 in) in height, making it the smallest member of the penguin family.

During the breeding season, penguins gather in large colonies. Year after year they return to the same rookery, where they take part in courtship displays - proudly extending their wings and pointing their bills skywards.

The female emperor penguin lays one egg at a time, which is carried around on the feet of the male while the female feeds at sea. Even after it has hatched, the young bird will ride on its father's feet until it is able to fend for itself.

There are 18 species of penguins in total, all of which inhabit the southern half of the world. They tend to breed near the equator on the Galapagos Islands, on the coasts of southern South America and Africa, in Australia and New Zealand, and on various islands of the southern oceans. Only two species, the adelie and the emperor, breed in Antarctica.

The kakapo (or owl parrot) is one of the many flightless birds of New Zealand.

The largest penguin is the emperor, which is also the world's largest sea bird. It stands about 1.2 metres (4 ft) tall, and can weigh up to 40 kilograms (90 lb). Most penguins feed on small crustaceans and fish near the water's surface, but the mighty emperor can descend as far as 260 metres (850 ft).

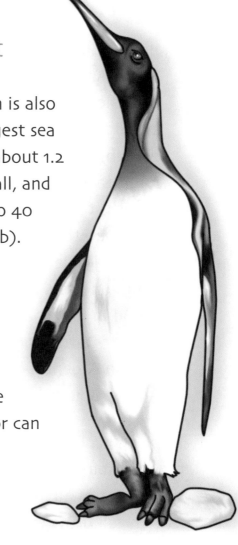

The penguin's flipper-like wings help it to 'porpoise' out of the water.

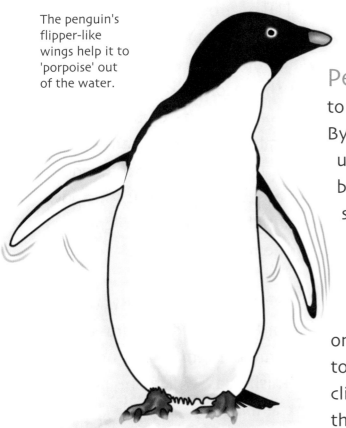

Penguins make up for their inability to fly with their excellent swimming skills. By 'porpoising' (swimming several metres under water and then thrusting into the air before re-submerging) they can reach speeds of up to 40 kilometres (25 miles) per hour.

Penguins come ashore by waddling onto beaches or by vaulting out of the surf to land upright on ice or rocks. They can climb steep slopes and often toboggan on their bellies over the snow.

Rheas, found only in South America, are rather like ostriches. Although their wings are bigger than those of an ostrich, they are still unable to fly. It takes young rheas just six months to reach adult size. There are three species of rhea: the long-billed rhea and the common rhea, which are both found in Brazil, and the slightly smaller Darwin's rhea, which lives in Argentina and the Andes Mountains.

Possibly the best known of all flightless birds is the African ostrich - the largest of all living birds. A male ostrich can grow to a height of 3 metres (10 ft) and weigh up to 150 kg (330 lb). An ostrich egg is yellowish white in colour and weighs about 1 kg (2.2 lb).

Although an ostrich cannot fly, it can run very fast - in fact it is the fastest creature on two legs. It can take strides of up to 3.5 metres (12 ft), and can run up to 50 kilometres (30 miles) per hour for 15 minutes at a time.

The ostrich can take strides of up to 3.5 metres (12 ft).

The kiwi gets its name from its shrill cry 'kee-wi, kee-wi'. It has no tail and its small, almost non-existent wings are hidden under its feathers. Several species of kiwi are found in New Zealand. There are 3 types of common, or brown kiwi and two types of spotted kiwi - the great spotted (or large grey) and the little spotted (or little grey).

A fully grown emu stands 1.5 metres (4.92 ft) high and may weigh up to 160 kilograms (353 lb). It is the second largest bird in the world and is quite common in Australia. As the emu can run very fast it usually flees when danger threatens but, if caught, this powerful fighter will kick violently at its enemy.

An emu's nest consists of a bed of trampled-down grass. In the autumn, the female lays up to ten greenish eggs, which are incubated by the male.

Man's Best Friend

Basenjis are the only dogs that do not bark. They were once used in central Africa as hunting dogs. The average height of a basenji is 43 centimetres (17 in) at the shoulder and it weighs about 11 kilograms (24 lb).

The rottweiler comes from Germany, where it was once used for herding cattle. It is a muscular animal with a large head and an average height of about 63 centimetres (25 in) at the shoulder. Rottweilers make excellent guard dogs and are very faithful.

The British bulldog was bred originally for the barbaric practice of bull-baiting, whereby the dog was trained to grab a bull by the nose and hang on at all costs. Fortunately bull-baiting was banned in 1835 and the bulldog is now a good-natured pet.

The labrador was originally trained as a hunting dog in the 19th century in New-foundland, Canada.

Golden Labrador

The chihuahua originates from Mexico. It is the world's smallest breed of dog, ranging in weight from 0.5 - 2.7 kilograms (1 - 6 lb), and standing about 13 centimetres (5 in) at the shoulder.

Although the bloodhound is often thought of as a police dog, because of its keen sense of smell, it was once bred as a hunting dog. Christopher Columbus took blood-hounds on his voyages to the New World, using them to seek out ambushes laid by the Native Americans.

As its name suggests, the Pekinese gets its name from the city of Peking (now Beijing) in China. When the British occupied the Summer Palace in Peking in 1860, they discovered five of these small dogs. One was presented to Queen Victoria and the rest were kept by the Duke of Richmond. Although some dogs were bred from these animals the breed did not become popular in Europe until the end of the 19th century, when more were imported from China. The Chinese name for this breed, means 'the lion dog'.

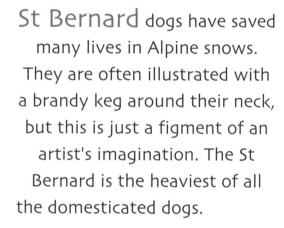

St Bernard dogs have saved many lives in Alpine snows. They are often illustrated with a brandy keg around their neck, but this is just a figment of an artist's imagination. The St Bernard is the heaviest of all the domesticated dogs.

The name 'dachshund' is German for 'badger dog', and that was the original purpose of this breed - to hunt badgers. Fortunately it is no longer used for this practice.

The chow chow is the only breed of dog with a blue tongue. It was used for centuries in China to hunt game, and is also depicted on pottery of the Han Dynasty.

The whippet, most likely a cross between a small English greyhound and a terrier, is thought to be the fastest domestic animal of its weight. With its long legs and streamlined body, the whippet can run up to 55 kilometres (34 miles) per hour.

Alsatians are used a great deal as police dogs, dogs for the blind and guard dogs. They originate from Germany and are often called German shepherds as they were once used for herding sheep and cattle.

In days gone by there were rather a lot of wolves in Russia, so hunters used borzoi dogs to reduce the numbers. Yet in spite of its history as a hunting dog, the borzoi makes a very affectionate pet.

Apart from being an affectionate pet, the collie is also used for herding sheep and cattle. It has a flat skull, a pointed muzzle and a long coat.

Animals in War

As war is a human problem, we forget the involvement of animals during such conflict. Many creatures have shown endurance, courage and devotion to duty far beyond that shown by man.

Many creatures that helped man during the First and Second World Wars have been awarded a Dicken Medal, the animal equivalent of the Victoria Cross medal for bravery.

Possibly the most famous pigeon to win the Dicken Medal was White Vision. In October 1943 White Vision delivered a message giving the position of a flying boat that had crashed near the Hebrides. The search for survivors had been called off, but with the arrival of the pigeon's message, the search was resumed and the crew was rescued.

The only cat to receive the Dicken Medal was Simon, who served on HMS Amethyst during the Second World War. Simon disposed of rats on board the ship, even after he had been wounded by shell blast.

The Carthaginian
General Hannibal crossed the Alps with his army in 218 BC, using elephants to carry the heavy loads. When he fought against Rome, he used the same elephants in his front line to shield his troops.

During the Second World War, a pointer dog called Judy became the only Japanese prisoner-of-war with four legs. Judy was the mascot of the gunboat HMS Grasshopper, and her adventures after the vessel sank in the South China Sea are astounding.

After Judy was rescued from the sunken vessel, she lived with British prisoners-of-war for several years. Much of her time was spent catching lizards and other small creatures, which she took to to the prisoners who were extremely grateful for such supplements to their meagre food rations.

The service of many other animals in wartime has not been officially recognised, but to them we owe a great deal for their gallantry and devotion to duty during some of the most appalling conditions that Man has created.

When troops once tried to attack Rome, a flock of geese raised the alarm with their calls. The guards were alerted and the city was saved.

Many animal mascots were kept by troops during the Second World War. One of the most unusual was a Syrian brown bear called Voytek.

Voytek had been sold to the 22nd Transport Company of the Polish 2nd Corps by a Persian boy in 1942. The bear stayed with the unit until the end of the war. He became quite a handful and the soldiers never knew what sort of prank he would get up to next. But in spite of his antics, Voytek proved to be a useful addition to the Polish forces, for he often helped with the unloading of munitions. He was so useful that the company badge was redesigned to show a bear carrying a shell.

Vanishing Animals

As people use more and more of the world's land for building, farming and roads, the places where animals live (their habitats) become smaller and smaller. This means that the number of animals in the world is decreasing rapidly. Hunting of certain animals is also reducing their numbers. If we do not do something to stop this, many species will disappear altogether. Some are already extinct and many more are threatened with extinction.

Only a few thousand mountain gorillas still live in Africa. Although it is large and powerful, the mountain gorilla is shy and does not cause harm unless angered. An adult male may reach a height of almost two metres (6.6 ft) and weigh up to 200 kilograms (440 lb). It feeds on fruit and vegetables and lives in groups.

The solenodon is a rat-like creature about 20 inches in length. It feeds on insects, small mammals and lizards. Only 2 species of solenodon remain – Cuban solenodon and the Haitian solenodon. Both are in danger of extinction.

Although it looks like a bear, the giant panda actually belongs to the same family as the raccoon. It can be found in the bamboo forests of south-west China, and is today greatly en-dangered. Tree-cutting and hunting have reduced panda numbers so much that the animal is now strictly protected. It is estimated that there are just 1500 pandas living in the wild, most of them in wildlife reserves.

The black-footed ferret is probably the rarest wild animal in North America. In 1982 the last surviving group of wild black-footed ferrets consisted of only 60 animals. They were immediately put under protection and by 1984 the number increased to 129. Sadly, a year later, they were almost wiped out by disease. The last 31 were captured and placed in wildlife reserves. When the numbers increased to over 300, some were released back into the wild. One of the reasons why the black-footed ferret is struggling to survive is because the prairie dog - one of its main sources of food - has been nearly wiped out by ranchers (who consider the dog a pest and a threat to their livestock).

The indri is the largest member of the lemur family, which is found only on the island of Madagascar in the Indian Ocean. It lives in the mountain forests and feeds mainly on leaves.

All tigers are in danger. The largest is the Siberian tiger, which roamed freely across Siberia, Mongolia, Manchuria and Korea. Sadly, its numbers have been drastically reduced through hunting.

All five members of the rhinoceros family are under threat. In addition to the Javan rhinoceros, there is the great Indian rhinoceros, the black rhinoceros, the white rhinoceros and the Sumatran rhinoceros. All of these are hunted for their horn, which is believed by some to contain powerful medicinal properties. The horn is made of compacted hair-like fibres called keratin.

Natural Wonders of the World

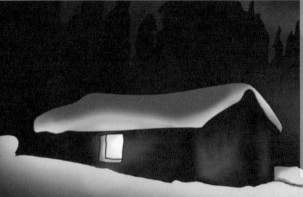

Strange lights can be seen near the North and South poles. The lights in the north are known as aurora borealis and those in the south are known as aurora australis. They are caused by electricity which is created when discharges from the sun enter the Earth's magnetic field.

One of the most famous of all the world's natural wonders is the USA's Grand Canyon. This great split in the planet's surface is some 446 km (277 miles) long, 6 - 29 km (4 - 18 miles) wide and 1.6 km (1 mile) deep. The canyon was formed by water over millions of years, as the Colorado River ate its way through the earth. The first white men to see it were Spanish explorers in 1540. But the canyon was explored properly after 300 years, when Major John Powell took a team of rowing boats through the dangerous rapids. In 1971, the river was properly mapped when space satellites started taking photographs of the region. The beautiful canyon is also called 'The Gateway to Heaven' by the local Hopi Indians.

On Mount Auyantepui, Venezuela, there is one of the most spectacular natural wonders of the world: Angel Falls. At a height of 979 metres (3212 ft), it is the world's highest waterfall.

Ayers Rock is an enormous stone in the Australian outback, near Alice Springs. It measures 9.6 km (6 miles) around its base, and has been called 'the biggest pebble in the world'. It was 'discovered' by an Englishman, W.G. Gosse, in 1873 and named after the Prime Minister of Australia, Sir Henry Ayers, but ownership has now been returned to the Aboriginal people. It consists of red sandstone that looks bright crimson at sunrise and purple at sunset. The colours change frequently through all shades of orange and red.

Giant's Causeway, on the Antrim coast of Northern Ireland, consists of thousands of columns of rock. Mostly irregular hexagons, the columns reach a maximum height of 6 m (20 ft), and a diameter of 50 cm (20 in). The causeway runs for 5 km (3 miles) along the coast and was formed by the cooling and contraction of a lava flow millions of years ago.

The Age of the Dinosaur

The largest dinosaur eggs ever found were those of the hypselosaurus, which lived some 80 million years ago. The eggs, measuring 300 x 255 millimetres (11 x 10 in), were discovered in southern France in 1961.

Dinosaurs lived between 215 and 65 million years ago. During their existence they dominated life on Earth. Then, relatively quickly, the dinosaurs disappeared - most likely due to dramatic changes in the world's climate.

Many people believe dinosaurs were rather slow-moving creatures, but in fact some of them were very fast. Scientists believe that the ornithomimids, a family of ostrich-like creatures, could run much faster than the present-day ostrich.

One of the largest dinosaurs was the brachiosaurus, which lived 140 - 165 million years ago. It is thought to have been 21 metres (69 ft) long, and weighed up to 78 tonnes (170,000 lb). This plant-eating creature would have eaten about 400 kilograms (882 lb) of food per day!

The largest ever meat-eating creature was the tyrannosaurus, which lived some 70 million years ago. It weighed over 12,000 kg (26,400 lb) and measured some 15 metres (50 ft) from head to tail!

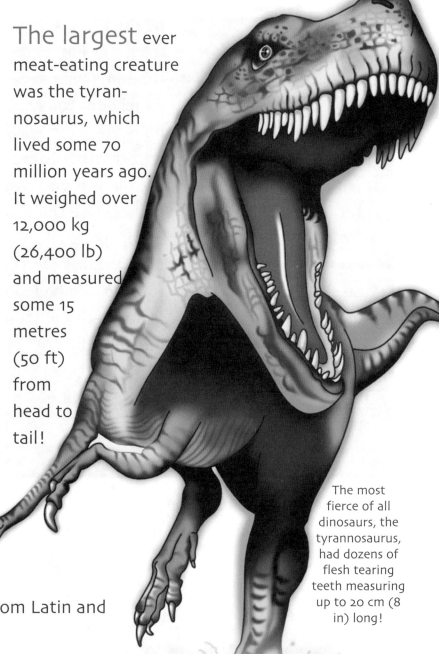

The most fierce of all dinosaurs, the tyrannosaurus, had dozens of flesh tearing teeth measuring up to 20 cm (8 in) long!

The word 'dinosaur' comes from Latin and Greek, meaning 'terrible lizard'.

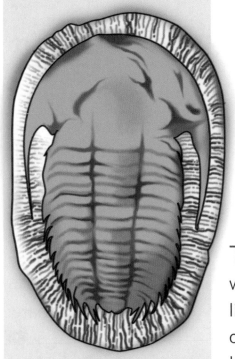

The proterosuchus was amazingly similar to its modern day descendant, the crocodile. It measured about 1.5 metres (4.9 ft) long, had a powerful jaw and a long tail. The proterosuchus also had very strong hind legs. It was from such creatures that many later animals developed the ability to walk on their hind legs.

All the knowledge that we have about dinosaurs comes from fossils. When a prehistoric animal died, the flesh would quickly decay. Layers of mud would build up gradually over the skeleton, eventually burying it. The weight of the top layers pressed the lower layers into rock, where minerals would eventually replace the bones of the skeleton, making an exact copy of the bones in stone. It is these stone remains that we call fossils.

The dimetrodon was a solar-powered lizard. It had a large fin on its back thought to be used for taking heat from the sun, in much the same way as a solar panel does today. As its body was warmer than that of other lizards, the dimetrodon was far more active than some other species. It measured about 3 metres (10 ft) long and had large front teeth for attacking and killing its prey.

The meat-eating megalosaurus was the first dinosaur to be identified by scientists. A fossil of this creature was described in 1677, but at the time no-one knew what it was. Further remains were found in 1818, but it was not until 1824 that a true description of the animal was made.

One of the smallest dinosaurs was the compsognathus which measured 60 cm (about 2 ft) from head to tail.

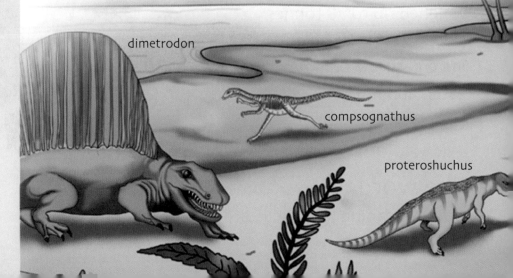

dimetrodon

compsognathus

proteroshuchus

No-one knows for certain what colour dinosaurs were. It is very likely that they diplayed a variety of colours, which may have been inflenced by the regions in which they lived - just like the animals of today.

The stegosaurus had the smallest brain of all the dinosaurs. The creature measured about six metres (20 ft) long. It had large bony plates along the whole length of its body and metre-long spikes at the end of its tail, yet its brain was only about the size of a walnut.

The triceratops had three horns, one over each eye and one on the nose. Although it averaged a height of 6 m (20 ft) and weighed as much as two fully grown elephants, the triceratops ate only plants.

Not all dinosaurs were meat-eaters; many were vegetarians. Scientists can tell which were which by examining fossils of their teeth and claws. Meat-eaters had long sharp teeth for tearing flesh, while plant-eaters had smaller teeth to chew leaves and branches. Some vegetarian dinosaurs were quite large; the plant-eating iguanodon measured up to 9.5 metres (31 ft) long. The biggest plant-eater was the diplodocus, which measured over 23 metres (75 ft) from nose to tail.

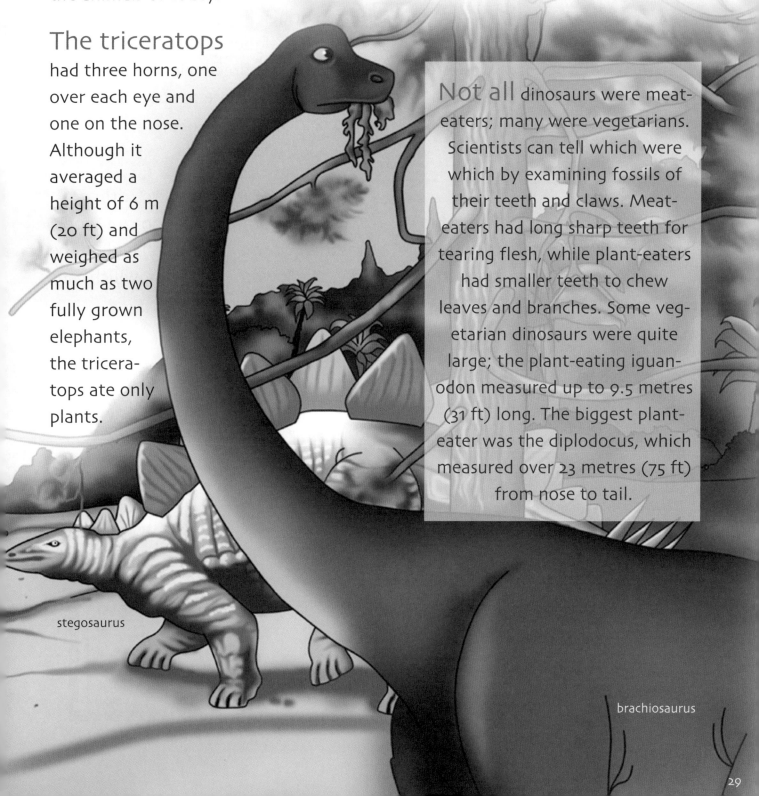

stegosaurus

brachiosaurus

A Question of Weather

There are three main categories of cloud: cumulus, stratus and cirrus. Cumulus are fluffy, like balls of cotton wool. Stratus are long and flat, and cirrus clouds are wispy or hazy.

The three types of cloud were named by Luke Howard, a British chemist whose hobby was the weather, in 1804.

In 1934 the wind speed on Mount Washington, in the USA, was recorded at 371 kilometres (231 miles) per hour.

Each type of cloud forms at different heights. To describe the different heights, another word is added to the three main names. The extra words are nimbo, strato, alto or cirro.

The highest clouds are cirrus, which can form from 5,000 to 13,700 metres (16,400 - 44,950 ft) high in the sky. The lowest are stratus, which can form right at ground level.

The windiest place on Earth is Commonwealth Bay, Antarctica. Here gales regularly reach 320 kilometres (200 miles) per hour.

Wind strength is measured by the Beaufort Scale. It was devised by Sir Francis Beaufort in 1806. The scale describes wind in thirteen stages ranging from 0, which is calm weather, to 12, which is a hurricane.

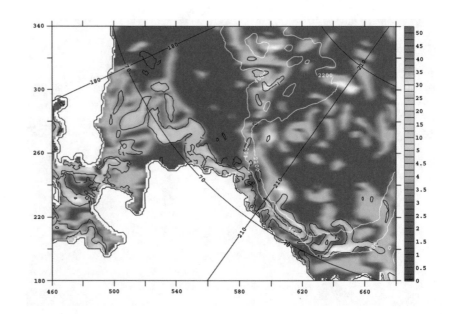

Types of Clouds

	Height (in metres)
Cirrus like fine strands of hair	5,000 - 13,700
Cirrocumulus this white cloud often shaped like small balls or ripples	5,000 - 13,700
Cirrostratus a thin white veil that covers all or most of the sky	5,000 - 13,700
Altostratus a grey or blue sheet of cloud made up of strands through which the sun filters	2,000 - 7,000
Nimbostratus a dark cloud layer accompanied by rain	900 - 3,000
Altocumulus small balls of fluffy cloud, either separate or joined up	2,000 - 7,000
Stratocumulus larger masses of fluffy cloud, either grey or white and often with darker patches	460 - 2,000
Cumulus fluffy clouds detached from other clouds	460 - 2,000
Cumulonimbus thick and large fluffy clouds, the bottom of which are usually dark	460 - 2,000
Stratus long, flat layers of cloud often accompanied by drizzle.	0 - 460

It is always wet on Mount Wai-'ale-'ale, on the Hawaiian island of Kauai. The mountain is constantly shrouded in mist, and receives over 11,000 millimetres (429 in) of rain annually. Strangely, on an island just a few miles away, only 500 millimetres (19.5 in) of rain fall each year.

Raindrops vary in size from about half a millimetre (.020 in) across for drops found in drizzle, up to eight millimetres (.312 in) across for thunderstorm drops.

Yuma, USA, boasts the most hours of sunshine: it remains sunny 90 per cent of the year.

On 7th September 1954, a shower of frogs fell on the people of Leicester, Massachusetts, USA. Similar showers of frogs and other creatures have been reported all over the world.

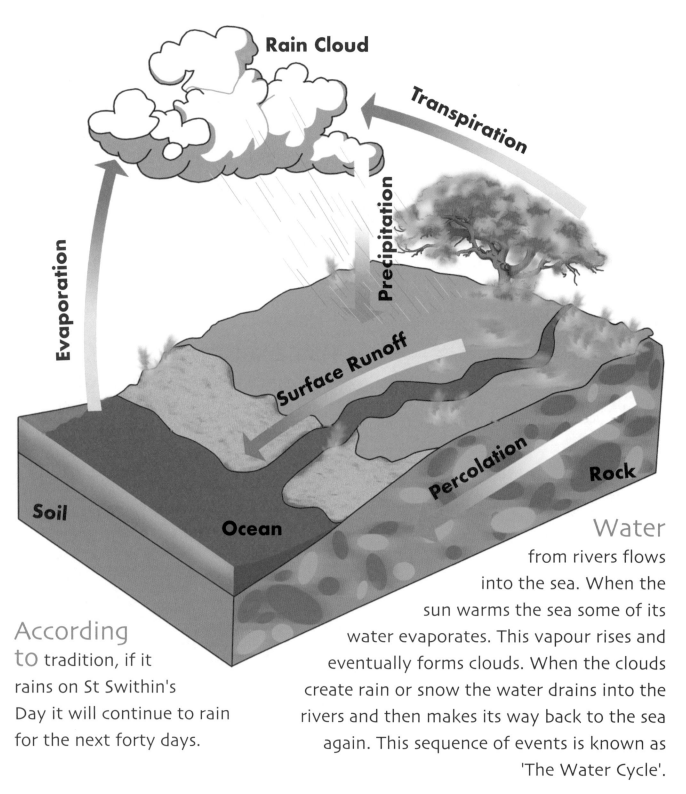

Rain Cloud

Transpiration

Evaporation

Precipitation

Surface Runoff

Percolation

Rock

Soil

Ocean

According to tradition, if it rains on St Swithin's Day it will continue to rain for the next forty days.

Water from rivers flows into the sea. When the sun warms the sea some of its water evaporates. This vapour rises and eventually forms clouds. When the clouds create rain or snow the water drains into the rivers and then makes its way back to the sea again. This sequence of events is known as 'The Water Cycle'.

In Torero, Uganda, thunder occurs for some 250 days of the year.

In 1894 a turtle encased in ice fell to the ground during a hailstorm over the Mississippi area of the USA.

On 14th April 1986, enormous hailstones killed over 90 people in Bangladesh. The hailstones reportedly weighed over one kilogram (2.2 lb) each.

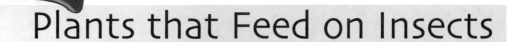

Plants that Feed on Insects

Several plants catch and 'eat' insects. Known as carnivorous plants, they include various types of flowering plants and fungi. Some carnivorous plants have even been known to trap and digest small frogs and birds!

A particularly ingenious way of catching food is performed by the pitcher plant. To attract insects, the plant produces a honey-like substance. Just below the honey (on the inside of the pitcher) the walls are very waxy, so the insect slides in. Inside the pitcher are tiny spines which stop the creature from escaping.

The Venus's Flytrap of North America is a popular house plant. When insects land between the leaves, the leaves snap shut (spikes on the leaves stop the insect from escaping). When the creature has been digested by the plant, the leaves fly open and the body is thrown out.

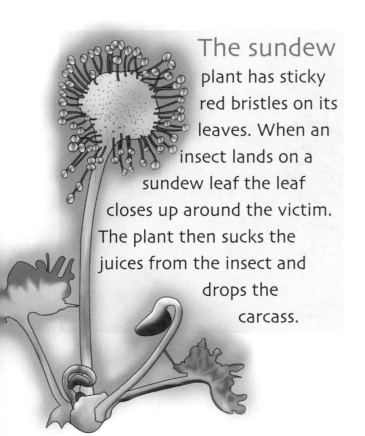

The sundew plant has sticky red bristles on its leaves. When an insect lands on a sundew leaf the leaf closes up around the victim. The plant then sucks the juices from the insect and drops the carcass.

Another carnivorous plant is the bladderwort. This aquatic plant has no roots, but floats just below the surface of water. Along the plant are small 'bladders' which puff out and suck in water and prey. Once a creature has found its way into one of these bladders, it cannot get out.

Snare traps are found in carnivorous fungi. One type of fungus has a trap that resembles a small lasso with three segments around the loop. When triggered, the segments bulge out to capture the victim, most likely a worm. The fungus then grows into the prey and digests it.

Trees of all Shapes and Sizes

There are three main groups of trees: conifers, broadleaves and palms. But trees can also be divided into two types: evergreens and deciduous. Deciduous trees lose their leaves in winter whereas evergreens, as their name suggests, keep their leaves all through the year.

All trees have leaves, but the quantity and type of leaf varies. The purpose of most leaves is to produce food, through photosynthesis. During this process, leaves absorb energy from the sun, turning carbon dioxide (a gas in the air) and water and minerals (in the ground) into a nutritious sap that flows upwards through the tree.

The purpose of roots is two-fold. Firstly, they anchor the tree to the ground so it is not easily blown over. Secondly, they draw up water and minerals from the soil.

Trees can live longer than any other plant or creature. The oldest tree in the world is a bristlecone pine, which grows in the White Mountains of the USA. It is over 4,700 years old.

A giant sequoia tree in the Sequoia National Park, California, is also the biggest living thing in the world. It is over 83 metres (272 ft) tall and has a circumference of more than 25 metres (82 ft).

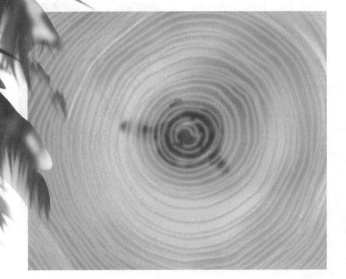

During each year of a tree's growth its trunk becomes thicker. When a tree is cut down, these growth periods can be seen clearly as a series of rings. The number of rings reveals the age of the tree. By analysing the thickness of the rings one can also determine what the weather was like during each year of growth.

Quinine, a medicine used in the treatment of malaria, comes from the bark of the cinchona tree in South America. Centuries ago local Indians discovered that by chewing the bark they could be free of the disease. In 1630 the Indians passed on this secret to some Jesuit priests, but it was not until 1820 that a method for removing the quinine from the bark was discovered.

The seed, or nut, of the coco de mer palm tree is the largest in the world and can weigh up to 22 kg (48 lb). Coco de mer seeds were known of long before the actual tree. They were often washed up on beaches in Asia and no-one knew what they were or where they had come from. The coco de mer palm was eventually discovered in the Seychelle islands of the Indian Ocean, the only place where this particular tree grows.

Amazing But True

In medieval times women used to store their tears in jars while their husbands were away fighting in the Crusades. The amount of tears collected was a symbol of the woman's love and devotion to her husband. Many women cheated by filling the jars with salt water!

According to the judges of a cookery contest in Pomona, California, worms taste like Shredded Wheat.

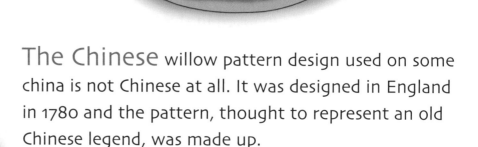

The Chinese willow pattern design used on some china is not Chinese at all. It was designed in England in 1780 and the pattern, thought to represent an old Chinese legend, was made up.

In accordance with the terms of her will, Margaret Thompson (who died in 1716) was buried in snuff (a finely powdered tobacco). At her funeral young girls distributed snuff to the mourners to cheer them up.

About 400 newspapers can be made from the wood pulp of one tree.

The great French general Napoleon Bonaparte was afraid of cats.

The town of Berwick-on-Tweed is officially still at war with Germany. When war was declared in 1939 no-one could decide whether Berwick was in Scotland or England, so it was mentioned separately in the declaration of war. There was not, however, any mention of Berwick in the peace treaty - so it would seem that Berwick is still at war!

To make just one spoonful of honey, bees have to visit about 5000 flowers.

The great ballet dancers Dame Margot Fonteyn (1919-91) and Rudolf Nureyev (1938-93) once received 89 curtain calls after a performance of Swan Lake.

Crowds of people who gathered to observe an eclipse in Milan in 1860 cried, "Long live the astronomers," as they believed that the astronomers had actually caused the eclipse themselves.

In April 1931, P.L. Wingo started a journey from California, USA, to Istanbul, Turkey. The trip took 19 months to complete, for Wingo walked all the way - backwards!

At least 7,500 varieties of apple are grown worldwide.

George I, who was King of England from 1715 to 1727, could not speak English - only German.

The sets of some of the great Hollywood cowboy films were only 7/8 the normal size, so that the actors appeared larger than life.

They Were First

The first policewoman was Mrs. Alice Wells, who worked for the Los Angeles Police Department in 1910.

The world's first photograph was taken by the French inventor Joseph Nicephore Niepce in 1822. Niepce also developed an early combustion engine, the pyreolophore.

The first British monarch to travel by train was Queen Victoria. On 13th June 1842, she and her husband Albert travelled from Slough to Paddington on the Great Western Railway.

The first doll's house was made for Duke Albrecht V of Bavaria in 1558.

The first known rickshaw was invented by the Reverend Jonathan Scobie, to escort his wife around Yokohama, Japan.

The first passenger underground railway opened in London on 10th January 1863; it ran from Paddington to Farringdon station. With over 400 kilometres (250 miles) of routes, the London Underground remains the longest underground system in the world.

The first game of snooker was invented by Sir Neville Chamberlain, when he was serving with the British Army in India in 1875.

The first guide dog for the blind was trained in Germany in 1916. The idea came from a Dr. Gorlitz, when he saw his dog fetch a blind patient's walking stick. The dog led the patient across the lawn of the hospital and the doctor decided to train other dogs to help the blind.

The first person to wear a top hat in public was James Hetherington. Such a large crowd gathered around him that some people fainted in the crush and one person was injured. The police arrested Hetherington and fined him £50 for disturbing the peace.

The first ambulance was designed by Baron Dominique Jean Larrey. He was Napoleon's personal surgeon and the ambulances were used to carry wounded men from the battlefield during Napoleon's Italian campaign of 1796.

The first refrigerator
for use in the home was the Domelre, manufactured in the USA in 1913.

The first milk bottles
were those used by Echo Farms Dairy of New York, in 1879.

The first escalator
was installed on Coney Island, New York, in 1896.

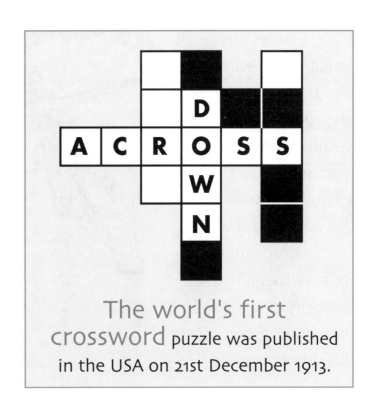

The world's first crossword puzzle was published in the USA on 21st December 1913.

Inventions

The telephone was invented because Alexander Graham Bell misread a report about the work of a German physicist, Hermann von Helmholz. Helmholz had made tuning forks vibrate by passing electricity through them. Bell thought that human speech had been transmitted and immediately set out to invent his own system of speech transmission. He finally succeeded on 10th March 1876 and the invention, which is now an important part of everyday life, came into being.

Many inventions were the result of accidents. One such invention was dry cleaning, developed by Jean-Baptiste-Jolly in 1825. He did so by accidentally knocking over an oil lamp. He then discovered that the parts of the table-cloth on which the oil had spilled were free of stains - he had discovered the basic principle of dry-cleaning.

The first American President, George Washington, once invented a special device for sowing seed.

Leonardo da Vinci, chiefly known for his art, has been described as one of the greatest inventors of all time. He drew designs for a parachute, a submarine, tanks, weapons of war and a glider. Unfortunately he was too far ahead of his time and most of his ideas did not actually come into being until long after his death.

Some of the greatest discoveries in electricity made in the 19th century were the result of work done by Michael Faraday. In 1821 he became the first person to make an electric motor. He also experimented in other areas and was the first to turn gas into a liquid by applying pressure.

One of the most important inventions of all time was the wheel. But its origins are lost in the mists of time, so no-one knows who invented it. It is quite likely that the wheel was developed over a long period by various people. The first wheels were probably cut-down tree trunks used as rollers.

It is said that the swivel chair, used in offices, barbers' shops and so on, was invented by the American President Thomas Jefferson.

Samuel Morse gave the first public demonstration of his code - enabling ships at sea to communicate with one another on 4th September 1837. He invented it after overhearing a passenger on board a ship suggest it would be useful if ships could communicate between themselves and with land bases. He immediately retired to his cabin and invented his code.

Today, Alfred Nobel is best known for the various prizes that bear his name. But he was also the inventor of dynamite, back in 1867. He did a lot of work on explosives and was called 'the merchant of death'. This upset Nobel greatly and he then spent a lot of time working for world peace.

The brothers Ladislao and Goerg Biro are usually associated with the invention of the ball-point pen. In fact they simply improved an idea that had been invented 50 years previously, by an American called John Loud.

It's Named After...

The majestic Eiffel Tower, in Paris, is named after the French engineer Alexandre-Gustave Eiffel, who built it for the Paris Exhibition of 1889.

The Fahrenheit temperature scale gets its name from the German scientist who invented it, Gabriel Daniel Fahrenheit.

A silhouette drawing is an outline of the subject filled in with black. The first known person to use this technique was Etienne de Silhouette, an 18th century French politician known for his meanness. To save money, de Silhouette would cut out decorations from black pieces of paper. Using the same black paper, he began making black portraits of people to earn extra money. Cut-outs such as these were first put on public display at an exhibition in 1759.

The word Juggernaut means 'any terrible force, especially one that destroys or that demands complete self-sacrifice'. Today the word is commonly used to describe the large trucks that travel on our roads. They can measure up to 20 metres (65 feet) in length, boast up to eighteen wheels and weigh up to a staggering 36,287 kilograms (80,000 lb).

The Catherine wheel is a popular firework. It is named after St Catherine, who was killed after being tied to a wheel which was then rolled down a hill.

A dunce is a fool, and yet the word comes from the name of a clever man. He was John Duns Scotus, a philosopher and religious teacher. After his death many said Scotus' teachings were stupid, and people who supported his ideas became known as 'dunsers'. It was not long before 'dunser' was shortened to 'dunce'.

People sometimes say: "It's a load of codswallop" when they think something is rubbish. The word 'codswallop' comes from an American called Hiram Codd. Towards the end of the 19th century he invented a special bottle that kept the fizz in lemonade. The liquid in a Codd bottle became known as 'Codd's wallop' ('wallop' being a slang word for beer). As it was generally regarded that beer was a better drink than lemonade, anything that was not very good became known as codswallop.

We often hear about problems caused by hooligans. The word 'hooligan' comes from the name Hoolihan, the surname of a rowdy Irish family who lived in London at the end of the 19th century. As stories about their activities spread around the country, the name changed to Hooligan and it has stuck as a term for anyone who behaves badly.

Anything large is often called jumbo, like a jumbo jet. The name originates from an exceptionally large elephant called Jumbo. Jumbo lived during the mid-19th century, first in Paris and then at London Zoo.

The luxury Pullman coaches, used by many railway companies, were first thought of by George Mortimer Pullman in 1859 and they have borne his name ever since.

The Yale lock is named after its inventor, the American locksmith Linus Yale Jnr.

The electrical term 'volt' comes from the Italian physicist and pioneer of electrical science, Alessandro Volta.

Breakthroughs in Medicine

Alexander Fleming's laboratory at St Mary's Hospital, London, was rather cluttered. His various experiments with bacteria lay everywhere. One day in 1921 he spotted that one of the dishes of bacteria had gone mouldy. When he looked closer he saw that all around the mould the bacteria had disappeared. He scraped up the mould and did some further work on it. It turned out that he had discovered penicillin and today millions of people owe their lives to this discovery.

In 1921 Frederick Banting and Charles Best began researching the disease of diabetes. They found that the pancreas produced a chemical called insulin. When insulin from healthy animals was injected into others with diabetes, they found that it halted the disease. They injected it into a human for the first time in 1922 and the result was a complete success.

The treatment of diabetes took a great leap in 1955 when Frederick Sanger discovered the make-up of insulin. This made it possible to make insulin chemically instead of taking it from animals.

Louis Pasteur first discovered germs when studying fermentation in wine. He found that the germs could be destroyed by heat. This process is now called pasteurisation.

Diphtheria once caused immense suffering and even death. Today it is almost unknown thanks to a serum developed by Emil von Behring in 1890.

The circulation of blood through our bodies was a complete mystery until William Harvey published his findings in 1628. It has been said that modern medicine started at this point.

She was sick, poor and worked in bad conditions, yet Madame Curie was dedicated to her work. She devoted most of her life to obtaining pure radium, an element that she and her husband Pierre had discovered. After almost four years of non-stop work, she finally succeeded in obtaining one three-hundredth of an ounce in 1902. It was discovered that radium could destroy diseased body cells and could attack certain forms of cancer. The Curies could have patented radium and made a fortune, but Madame Curie decided that her discovery should be donated to the benefit of all.

When he was just a small boy Louis Pasteur saw a rabid dog biting people. In later life he found a cure for rabies, the disease that causes madness in animals and death to humans.

The first human-to-human heart transplant was performed by the South African surgeon Dr Christiaan Barnard, in December 1967.

In the 18th century John Hunter provided an immense amount of knowledge on how the body works by dissecting the bodies of both humans and animals.

During an outbreak of smallpox in England in the late 17th century, Edward Jenner remembered the old wives' tale that a milkmaid who caught cowpox would never suffer with smallpox. He looked into this and decided that an injection of cowpox might immunise against smallpox. Jenner was proved right and it was not long before his idea of vaccination was widely used.

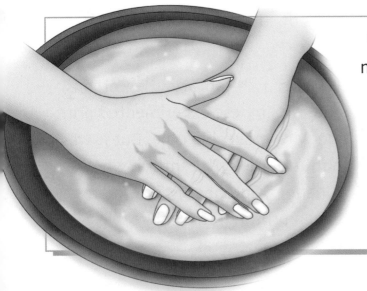

One of the greatest breakthroughs in medicine was also one of the simplest. In 1847 Ignaz Semmelweis reduced deaths in childbirth by simply washing his hands in chlorinated lime, an early antiseptic solution, before treating his patients. Joseph Lister, in 1865, was the first to use antiseptics for surgery.

The Marvel of Books

Books are the most important of man's possessions, for they contain all knowledge acquired since the dawn of civilisation. The wisdom of the ancients, man's achievements and failures, his beliefs and disbeliefs, are all contained in books.

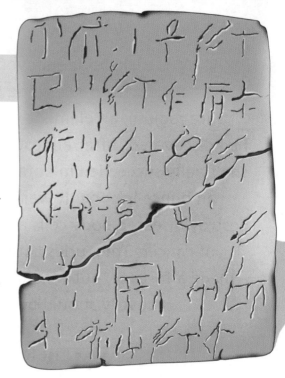

The first printing of a book was done with wooden blocks. The earliest book known to have been produced by this method is a Buddhist scroll, printed in China in the year 868.

Romans were the first to fasten together sheets of parchment on one edge, producing the shape of the book as we know it today.

Gutenberg's Press was hand-operated. It took him 3 years to produce 190 copies of the Gutenberg Bible, published in 1455.

The first known written records consisted of clay tablets dating from the 4th century BC. Pieces of reed were used as pens to write on the clay while it was damp. Writing was a swift job in those days, as it was impossible to write on the clay once it had dried.

Ashurbanipal, who was King of Syria around 650 BC, had a library of 20,000 clay tablet books on all sorts of subjects.

In the 11th century, the Koreans and the Chinese experimented printing with moveable type. But it was not until the 15th century, when Johannes Gutenberg of Germany began printing, that moveable type came into general use.

The ancient Egyptians produced their books on scrolls of papyrus, brittle sheets of paper-like material made from the pith of the papyrus plant (from which we get the word 'paper').

In ancient China silk was used as a writing material. In AD 105, a court official, Ts'ai Lun, suggested writing on a solid mixture of pounded rags and wood pulp - thought to be the first use of paper.

From the 2nd century BC, parchment replaced papyrus as the writing material of choice. Parchment is made from animal skins and proved far stronger than papyrus.

Possibly the most beautiful book in the world is The Book of Kells. It was produced by monks in the 9th century, on the Hebridean island of Iona. All but two of its 680 pages were illustrated over many years.

When Vikings invaded Iona in the year 806, some of the monks escaped to Ireland, taking the manuscript with them. Work continued on the book in Kells, in County Meath. Sadly, in 1006, the book was stolen. But the thieves were interested only in the gold and jewel-encrusted cover. They tore this off and buried the pages. Three months later the pages were recovered. In 1653 the book was moved to Dublin, where it remains to this day.

Before the days of printing, books could only be produced by handwriting each copy. This was a long and laborious process, so books were rare and expensive. The invention of printing meant that a book could be copied many times very quickly.

At one time religious books were incredibly costly to make and therefore extremely valuable, so they were kept in 'chained' libraries. Such libraries allowed people to read but stopped the books from being stolen, as they were literally chained to the shelves or desks. In spite of these precautions some books have been stolen - in the chained library of Wells Cathedral only the chains remain! There are still some chained libraries with their books intact in English churches. Among the most famous are the 17th-century library at Wimborne Minster in Dorset and the 16th-century library of St Wulfrum's Church in Grantham, Lincolnshire. The largest remaining chained library in the world is in Hereford Cathedral. It houses some 1500 books, some printed and some handwritten.

The first book printed in English was called Recuyell of the Historyes of Troy. Printed in Belgium in 1474, it was originally a French work on the history of Troy, which was translated into English by William Caxton. Two years later Caxton set up a printing press in London. On 18th November 1477, he published Dictes and Sayenges of the Philosophers, the first book printed in Britain.

In 1976 Ian Macdonald produced a very tiny book with a very long title. It was called 'A Three Point Type Catalogue In Use At Gleniffer Press', and it measured just 2.9 x 1.5 mm (0.11 x 0.05 cm) square. The book consisted of 30 pages containing the entire alphabet, with just one letter to a page, the title page and end papers. Nine years later the Gleniffer Press, which specialises in very small books, published the story Old King Cole in a book measuring just one millimetre (0.039 in) square!

Flags are much more than just pieces of coloured material - they have been at the forefront of many historical events. Flags have been fought for, torn, stoned and burned. Many people have died protecting the flag they love.

Early on the practical uses of flags became evident; they could identify a military force or officer, and even indicate tactical instructions on the battlefield. The armies of ancient Egypt carried poles bearing ribbons when they went into battle. Roman soldiers carried a vexilla, a square of coloured cloth hung from a pole.

The Indian flag depicts a blue wheel (a chakra), symbolising the cycle of life. The 24 spokes represent the hours in a day.

Flags as we know them today, however, are thought to be the creation of the Chinese, around 1100 BC.

In the 14th century a Spanish friar wrote what is believed to be the first book about flags. It was called 'Book of the Knowledge of All the Kingdoms, Lords and Lordships that are in the World'.

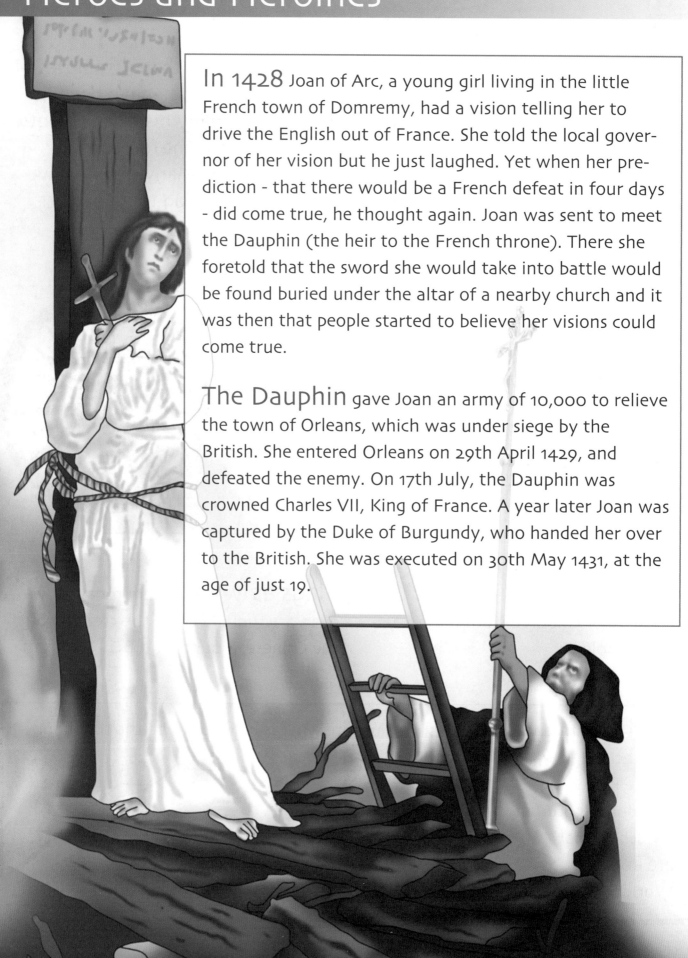

Heroes and Heroines

In 1428 Joan of Arc, a young girl living in the little French town of Domremy, had a vision telling her to drive the English out of France. She told the local governor of her vision but he just laughed. Yet when her prediction - that there would be a French defeat in four days - did come true, he thought again. Joan was sent to meet the Dauphin (the heir to the French throne). There she foretold that the sword she would take into battle would be found buried under the altar of a nearby church and it was then that people started to believe her visions could come true.

The Dauphin gave Joan an army of 10,000 to relieve the town of Orleans, which was under siege by the British. She entered Orleans on 29th April 1429, and defeated the enemy. On 17th July, the Dauphin was crowned Charles VII, King of France. A year later Joan was captured by the Duke of Burgundy, who handed her over to the British. She was executed on 30th May 1431, at the age of just 19.

Amy Johnson was the most famous woman of her time. In 1930, having never been abroad before, she left Croydon, England, to become the first woman to fly alone to Australia - only one man had flown the journey solo before. Her longest flight prior to this epic trip was from London to Hull. She had left England completely unknown, but on her arrival in Australia she became an international celebrity. In 1931 she made the first flight to Moscow in one day and in 1932 she flew to Cape Town in four days, beating her husband's record by 10 hours.

Davy Crockett died while fighting to save the Alamo in 1836. At that time Mexico regarded the American state of Texas as Mexican territory. When the Mexican army marched into San Antonio they found the Alamo, a missionary church, occupied by a band of Texans. The Mexicans, under the command of General Santa Anna, attacked. While Crockett and his men defended the church, other Texans organised the resistance that eventually saved Texas from Mexican rule.

On 7th September 1838, the steamship Forfarshire was shipwrecked on the Farne Islands off the coast of Northumberland. William Darling, the lighthouse-keeper, saw that some of the shipwrecked people had managed to scramble onto the rocks. He and his 23-year-old daughter, Grace, rowed through rough seas to rescue the survivors. The news of this gallant rescue spread like wildfire and Grace Darling became famous overnight. Her house in Bamburgh is now a museum.

Boadicea was the queen of the Iceni tribe in Britain when the Romans invaded in 43 BC. She and her followers decided to rebel against the might of Rome. As most Britons disliked the Roman rule, many other tribes joined the Iceni in their uprising.

They attacked the Romans and captured many of their strongholds, spurred on by the sight of Boadicea in her chariot urging the men into battle. But the Britons' triumph was short-lived, for the Romans eventually proved too powerful. As a result of Boadicea's stand, the Romans became less cruel towards the British, and the name of Boadicea has gone down in history as the fighting queen who defied the might of the Roman Empire.

Thomas Edward Lawrence, better known as Lawrence of Arabia, was a leader in an Arab revolt against the Turks. His actions drove the Turks out of Syria. For 19 months, from March 1917, Lawrence led the Arabs in raids. He lived with them and dressed as they did. The Arabs looked up to Lawrence as their leader and had great respect for his courage and determination.

Robin Hood was a legendary outlaw thought to have lived in Sherwood Forest, near Nottingham, during the Middle Ages. It may be that the character is based on the stories of many outlaws who frequented the British Isles at that time - or it could be that the whole story was simply made up. The legend tells of Robin and his band of merry men who robbed rich travellers and gave the money to the poor. He carried on his adventurous deeds until about 1346, when he is said to have died in Kirklees priory.

The Masters of Music

Wolfgang Amadeus Mozart is regarded by many as the greatest classical composer in history. Mozart's interest in music started at a very early age - he began playing the harpsichord at the age of three and gave his first public performance two years later. When he was six, he and his ten-year-old sister toured Europe giving performances. Mozart was born in Salzburg, Austria, in 1756, and died when he was only 35. During his short life he created more than 600 pieces of music. He wrote his first symphony when he was only eight and his first opera at the age of eleven.

The British composer Henry Purcell was only 18 when, in 1677, he was appointed Composer for the King's Violins.

Peter Ilyich Tchaikovsky was best known for his ballets Swan Lake (1876), Sleeping Beauty (1889) and The Nutcracker (1892), but he also wrote concertos, symphonies and many other pieces of music. Tchaikovsky was a rather unhappy person and much of his music has an air of sadness. He was born in Russia in 1840, and died of cholera in 1893.

George Frederick Handel was born in Halle, Germany, in 1685, but in 1726 he became a naturalised Englishman. Handel is best known for his English oratorios. His most famous work is undoubtedly the Messiah, which he wrote in 1742. Handel's popular Water Music and his Fireworks Music were both written for special occasions for the English royal court.

Handel's father disliked music, so as a young boy George had to smuggle a clavichord (a sort of small piano) into the attic where he practised secretly.

Johann Strauss and his son, also called Johann, had their own individual orchestras. Both father and son wrote a number of popular waltzes - Johann Jr. composed almost 500!

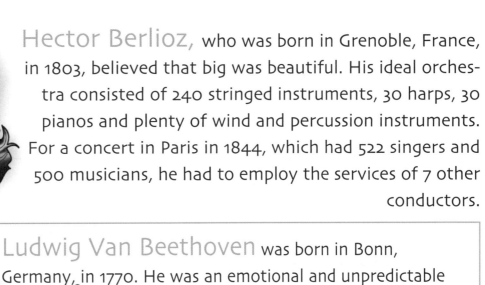

Hector Berlioz, who was born in Grenoble, France, in 1803, believed that big was beautiful. His ideal orchestra consisted of 240 stringed instruments, 30 harps, 30 pianos and plenty of wind and percussion instruments. For a concert in Paris in 1844, which had 522 singers and 500 musicians, he had to employ the services of 7 other conductors.

Ludwig Van Beethoven was born in Bonn, Germany, in 1770. He was an emotional and unpredictable man who was only 30 years old when he began to lose his hearing. Beethoven was completely deaf by the time he was 50, but that did not stop him from composing some of the most powerful music of all time. He wrote some superb symphonies but composed only one opera, Fidelio, first performed in 1805.

Johann Sebastian Bach (1685-1750) was a master of choral and instrumental music; over 1000 of his compositions survive even today. Several of his 20 children also became well-known composers.

Another 18th century German composer was Johann Melchior Molter, who wrote 169 symphonies.

Frederic François Chopin was one of the world's finest composers of classical piano music. His interest in music began very young, when he would try to copy his sister who was learning to play the piano. This triggered a natural gift for music and Chopin gave his first public concert when he was eight. He was born in Poland in 1810, but spent most of his life in France following a successful concert tour at the age of 19. Chopin died of tuberculosis in 1849.

The Austrian composer Franz Joseph Haydn was known as the 'father of the symphony'. He was largely self taught and yet he is regarded as one of the greatest composers of his time.

Making Unusual Music

The bows with which orchestral strings are played, such as those for the cello, double bass, or viola, are made of horsehair stretched over a slightly curved stick. The bows were developed over the years from simple archery-type bows, and reached their present forms in the late 18th century.

At the Jubilee Gardens in London, on 9th July 1988, an enormous set of Pan pipes was played. There were ten pipes in all, the smallest being over one metre (3.28 ft) in length and the longest an incredible three metres (9.8 ft).

The folk box zither of the Alps is a stringed instrument whereby up to 37 strings are stretched over a sound box. The four top strings provide the melody and the remainder are used to produce the accompaniment. The melody strings are plucked with the fingers or with a plectrum (a small piece of bone, plastic or other material).

The dulcimer is placed on the lap for playing. A small stick, held in the left hand, is moved up and down the strings to adjust the pitch, while the melody is plucked out by one finger of the right hand.

The jew's harp (or jaw's harp) is a very old instrument. Players of the harp grip the metal frame with their teeth and pluck the metal tongue with their fingers. Different twanging sounds are made by the player altering the shape of his or her mouth.

The Pan pipes consist of tubes of different lengths joined together. By blowing through the pipes it is possible to produce different notes; the longer the tube the lower the note. The Pan pipes are named after Pan, the Greek god of the woods, fields, sheep and shepherds. Shepherds used the pipes of Pan to pass the time while watching their flocks.

One of the earliest methods of making sounds was the bull-roarer. This is simply a string attached to a flat piece of wood. When the player whirls it around his head, the wood twists in the air to produce a buzzing sound. In days gone by Australian aborigines believed that the bull-roarer had magical properties.

The crumhorn was a reed instrument of the Middle Ages. Its name derives from the Old English word 'crump', which means crooked.

The serpent, which came into fashion in the 16th century, was made from two pieces of wood bound together. In Germany it was known as the 'snake tube' and people in the north of England called it the 'black pudding'.

The petrol drum is probably one of the strangest musical instruments ever invented. Yet this specially adapted tin drum produces beautiful sounds. The head of the drum is divided into a number of sections, which are beaten with a rubber stick to varying degrees, to produce different notes. Petrol drums are used by steel bands, which originated in the West Indies.

Although classed as a musical instrument, the kazoo is not particularly musical. Yet some marching bands use them a lot, as do some jazz bands. All the kazoo really does is alter a humming sound made by the player, rather like humming through a piece of tissue paper stretched over a comb. In 1975 a giant kazoo was made in Rochester, New York. Some two metres (6.5 ft) long and over a metre wide, it weighed 19.5 kilograms (43 lb) and took four people to play it!

Ancient Wonders of the World

The seven wonders of the world include the greatest feats of architecture and art as viewed by the ancient Greek and Roman writers. The Greek poet Antipater, circa 130 BC, was the first to list the wonders: the Pyramids of Egypt, the Mausoleum at Halicarnassus, the Hanging Gardens of Babylon, the Temple of Artemis, the Pharos of Alexandria, the Colossus of Rhodes and the Statue of Zeus.

The Temple of Artemis at Ephesus:

The Temple of Artemis (Diana), the goddess of the moon, was built at Ephesus in Turkey in 350 BC. It stood for 600 years until it was finally destroyed by the Goths in AD 263.

The Mausoleum at Halicarnassus:

Mausolus was the King of Caria. When he died, his wife, Queen Artemisia, had a magnificent tomb built for him at Halicarnassus (now Bodrum) in Turkey. It was finished in 325 BC.

Of the original 'seven wonders', only the pyramids remain intact. But there are, however, some remains of the Temple of Diana and the tomb of King Mausolus.

The Pyramids of Egypt:

The pyramids were built some 4000 years ago, on the west bank of the Nile near Memphis, as tombs for Egyptians kings and queens.

The Hanging Gardens of Babylon:
According to legend, King Nebuchadnezzar had the terraces of the city of Babylon filled with beautiful hanging plants to please his wife, Amytis. Babylon was an ancient city in Iraq and the gardens flourished around 600 BC.

The Colossus of Rhodes:
An enormous statue of the sun god Helios once spanned the harbour entrance at the island of Rhodes, in Greece. Known as the Colossus of Rhodes, measuring some 36 metres (120 ft) high, it was destroyed by an earthquake in 224 BC.

The Statue of Zeus at Olympia:
In the 5th century BC the sculptor Phidas built a marvellous statue of the supreme Greek god, Zeus. It was made of solid gold and ivory, and measured some 12 metres (40 ft) in height.

The Pharos of Alexandria:
On an island in the harbour of Alexandria, Egypt, stood the magnificent lighthouse known as the Pharos. The Pharos was made of solid marble and was the earliest known example of a lighthouse. Its light came from a fire which was reflected out to sea by curved mirrors. The Pharos was built in 270 BC but was destroyed by an earthquake in AD 1375.

The Great British Castle

The Romans were the first to build stone castles in Britain, but the best-known are those constructed in the Middle Ages, between 1100 and 1400. Some of the most elaborate castles were those built by King Edward I in Wales.

To protect their outer walls, many castles were surrounded by a moat (a water-filled ditch). Some castles used rivers as part of their moat, but most moats were man-made.

Many castles had posterns - secret ways of getting in and out of the castle without being seen by the enemy.

Possibly the most famous castle in Britain is the Tower of London. It was built by William the Conqueror, after he crossed the Channel to conquer England in 1066.

The oldest castle in England is Dover Castle. It was built on the site of a Roman lighthouse, perched on the cliffs above the town's harbour. Renovations over the centuries have included a Norman keep and a Saxon chapel.

The world's largest inhabited castle is Windsor Castle, Berkshire. It has been the home of British royalty for over 900 years.

Castles were often the sight of fearsome battles. One striking example is the 'leaning tower' of Caerphilly Castle in South Wales. It was damaged by cannonfire in the Middle Ages, and has leaned ever since.

A spiral staircase in a castle was always built to ascend clockwise. Any swordsman climbing the stairs would have his right arm against the central pillar making it harder to attack. The defender, coming down the stairs with the sword in his right hand, had much more freedom of movement.

To cross the moat there would be a drawbridge. This was a hinged bridge that could be raised when the castle was under attack.

The floor of the gatehouse (built over the gateway) was often full of small holes. These were used for dropping stones or other objects onto any enemies who tried to enter. To further reinforce the gateway, many castles had an outer wall, or barbican which screened the gate from attack.

The weakest part of a castle was the gateway, so special defences were devised to protect it. Most gateways had a metal grille called a portcullis. This could slide down to shut off the gateway. But it was not used just to keep enemies out - it would also trap them inside so they could be attacked more easily!

The European Union

The European Union –

previously known as the European Community – is an institutional framework for the construction of a united Europe. It was created after World War II to unite the nations of Europe economically so another war among them would be unthinkable. The EU currently has 15 member countries.

The Treaty

on EU was signed in Maastricht on 7th February 1992 and came into force on 1st November 1993. The European Community, which was essentially economic in aspiration and content, was transformed into the EU.

POPULATION	
In 2001, the population of the EU was almost 378 million.	
Austria	8.2
Belgium	10.3
Denmark	5.4
Finland	5.2
France	59.6
Germany	83
Greece	0.6
Ireland	3.8
Italy	57.7
Luxembourg	0.4
Netherlands	16
Portugal	10
Spain	40
Sweden	8.9
United Kingdom	59.6
Total	378.7

There are

currently eleven official languages of the European Union in number (Danish, Dutch, English, Finnish, French, German, Greek, Italian, Portuguese, Spanish and Swedish). Irish (Gaelic, "Gaeilge") is regarded as an official language where primary legislation (i.e. the Treaties) is concerned.

The EU

is based on the rule of law and democracy. Its Member States delegate sovereignty to common institutions representing the interests of the Union as a whole on questions of joint interest. All decisions and procedures are derived from the basic treaties ratified by the Member States.

The Community

pillar is run according to the traditional institutional procedures and governs the operations of the Commission, Parliament, the Council and the Court of Justice.

IMPORTANT DATES IN THE EU

1950 French foreign minister Robert Schuman proposes a plan to improve the growth of both France and Germany after World War II. The Schuman Plan was also designed to make war between the two countries impossible, as their main industries would be governed by one authority.

1952 The Schuman Plan results in the creation of the European Coal and Steel Community (ECSC). Italy, Belgium, the Netherlands and Luxembourg join the ECSC.

1957 The six countries set up the European Economic Community and the European Atomic Energy Community.

1973 The United Kingdom, Ireland and Denmark joined the European Economic Community and the number of countries has increased gradually ever since.

2001 The 2001 Intergovernmental Conference results in the Treaty of Nice.

YEAR OF JOINING THE EU:

FRANCE	1957
GERMANY	1957
ITALY	1957
NETHERLANDS	1957
BELGIUM	1957
LUXEMBOURG	1957
UNITED KINGDOM	1973
DENMARK	1973
IRELAND	1973
GREECE	1981
SPAIN	1986
PORTUGAL	1986
AUSTRIA	1995
FINLAND	1995
SWEDEN	1995

Principal objectives of the EU are:

● Establish European citizenship (Fundamental rights; Freedom of movement; Civil and political rights)
● Ensure freedom, security and justice (Cooperation in the field of Justice and Home Affairs)
● Promote economic and social progress (Single market; Euro, the common currency; Job creation; Regional development; Environmental protection).

Eleven of the EU member countries (Belgium, France, Germany, Italy, Spain, Portugal, Finland, Austria, the Netherlands, Ireland and Luxembourg) adopted a new common European currency, called the "euro," on January 1, 1999. The European Central Bank (ECB) is housed in Frankfurt, Germany.

Money

In ancient China spades were once used as money. Over hundreds of years the spades were replaced by models of spades. Often these had holes in them so they could be strung around the waist. Gradually the model spade was made smaller and smaller, until it was only a small piece of metal with a hole in it. This was the first true coin, and came into use in China around 1090 BC. The Chinese are also thought to be the first to have used paper money, back in the 9th century.

Spades were not the only objects to be used as money. Varying metal shapes, tea, salt, rice, cattle, sea shells and other important goods have all been used as money at one time or another.

Stones were once used as money on the island of Yap in the Pacific Ocean. Small amounts were stones with holes in them which were strung on wooden poles. Larger stones could not be moved, but as everyone on the island knew one another, it was not considered a problem.

China issued the largest ever paper money. The one kwan note, produced in 1368, measured 23 cm (9 in) by 33 cm (13 in).

In 1718 Sweden issued a four-dollar piece. It was about a centimetre thick and about 25 square centimetres (4 sq. in) and weighed several kilograms. It was the largest coin ever issued.

Sweden also holds the record for the heaviest coin ever minted, the ten-daler piece of 1644, which weighed almost 20 kilograms (44 lbs).

Up until 15th February 1971, British money consisted of pounds, shillings and pence. There were 12 pennies to a shilling and 20 shillings (or 240 pence) to a pound.

One of the first coins used in Britain was the silver penny, produced by King Offa of Mercia (757 - 796 AD). This silver penny remained the most common coin in Britain for over 600 years.

The first dollar coin was issued in Bohemia (now the Czech Republic) in the 16th century. The Count of Schilick made the coin from his own silver mine at Joachimsathal (Joachim's dale). He called it a 'Joachimsthaler', or 'dale-piece'. This was later shortened to 'thaler' from which 'dollar' originates.

When the French colonists in Canada were short of coins in 1685, they used playing cards as money.

Every country has its own type of money. Unfortunately the value of foreign money is not always the same as the money you use in our own country. This is why you have to exchange some of your money for a different currency when you go abroad.

From May 1841 to May 1842 the people of Mexico used bars of soap as money.

In 17th century England goldsmiths issued receipts for gold left in their care. The receipts were often exchanged instead of the gold and they eventually became the notes that we use today.

Washing, Ironing and Cleaning

One of the earliest washing machines was called the 'buck'. It was simply a large tub of water, into which the person washing the clothes would step and stomp on the dirty clothes until they were clean!

Another early washing machine was the 'dolly'. Like a small wooden stool with a pole on top, it would be placed in a wash bucket and turned from side to side, making the 'legs' of the 'stool' agitate the washing until clean.

In the 19th century a rocking machine was developed. This large box, attached to rockers, had to be rocked up and down to get the clothes clean.

By the early 20th century washing machines had improved but were still hand-operated. Often a mangle was attached so that excess water could be squeezed out of the clothes before they were hung out to dry.

In 1911 Frederick Louis Maytag, of Iowa, USA, developed an electric washing machine. His company, Maytag, became the world's largest producer of washing appliances.

Electric washing machines did not really become popular until after the Second World War and it was not until the early 1950s that they became common appliances in the home.

Long ago, heavy stone irons were used to press clothes. Then came the flat iron, which was made of metal, and was heated by the fire before use. The flat surface of the hot iron was wiped with beeswax to keep it smooth.

Before the vacuum cleaner was invented the best way to clean a carpet was to beat it. The carpet would be hung over a washing line and hit with a cane - hard and dusty work!

Vacuum cleaners came into use at the beginning of the 19th century. One early vacuum had to be operated by two people: one person worked a treadle up and down to make the sucking action, while the other person pushed the suction brush over the carpet.

By the end of the 19th century some flat irons were heated by methylated spirit, paraffin or gas in a special heater.

Box irons were like flat irons, only hollow. Hot coals or pieces of hot metal would be put into the 'box' to heat the iron.

Electric irons were first introduced in the early 20th century. They became increasingly popular as more and more homes became powered by electricity.

The first steam irons came on the market in the 1950s. The steam, or spray, dampens the cloth before ironing which is necessary with some materials.

Fashion Through the Ages

A popular outfit for men in the 16th century was the goose-belly. It originated in Spain and was basically a padded front piece in a doublet (a close-fitting jacket), creating an artificial paunch!

Right up until the 19th century it was common for people to keep the same clothes on day and night, until the garments wore out.

The word 'jeans' comes from the name of the city of Genoa in Italy. Genoan sailors used to wear trousers of a thick, canvas-like material. The French called them Genes, the French word for Genoa, and the name has stuck ever since.

In early Victorian times extremely full skirts were fashionable. They were supported by numerous petticoats, which were later replaced with a framework of hoops.

In the 15th century sleeves were separate garments that were laced onto the rest of the outfit.

Pyjamas developed from the everyday dress of men in Northern India. But the word 'pyjamas' is not Indian, it actually comes from Persia.

When Levi Strauss left his native Bavaria for a better life in the USA, he took with him some denim which he hoped to sell to gold prospectors for making tents. An old miner told him he should have brought trousers, as they were always wearing out under the tough mining conditions. Strauss then used the denim to make trousers, they became popular and are now known as jeans.

During medieval times it was fashionable to wear long-pointed shoes. Through the years the shoes were made longer and longer. Eventually the end of the toe had to be tied back to the top of the boot, to enable the wearer to walk without falling over his feet!

When gloves first appeared in Britain they were worn only by the rich. Gloves were a sign that the wearer did not have to work with his or her hands.

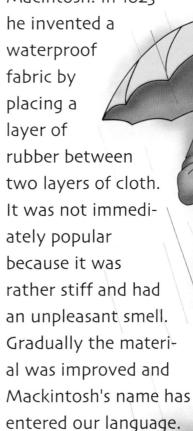

Wellington boots were named after the Duke of Wellington. In the Battle of Waterloo in 1815, Wellington wore long boots with no turnover at the top. After the battle people began to copy the duke and wore these boots for everyday use. Over the years they have changed and we now wear them just for wet or muddy conditions, but the name remains.

In medieval Paris, clothing manufacturers promoted their designs by sending dolls dressed in the latest styles to cities and courts throughout Europe.

In 1989 a company in Holland made a zip fastener that was 2,851 metres (9,354 ft) long. It had 2,565,900 teeth.

Raincoats are called mackintoshes, or 'macs' for short, after Charles Macintosh. In 1823 he invented a waterproof fabric by placing a layer of rubber between two layers of cloth. It was not immediately popular because it was rather stiff and had an unpleasant smell. Gradually the material was improved and Mackintosh's name has entered our language.

Around the World on a Plate

Every country in the world has a speciality food or meal. The meal usually associated with Japan, for instance, is sushi. Mostly sushi consists of raw fish served with small cakes of cold rice.

Moussaka, a traditional dish of Greece, consists of minced beef in a cheese sauce topped with sliced aubergines.

Paella is Spain's best known dish. This meal of chicken and seafood served with rice is cooked in a large shallow pan called a paelleria.

Strudel is thin pastry wrapped around a filling such as apple or mincemeat. It is a speciality of Austria and Germany.

The dish most closely associated with the USA is the hamburger. Yet it did not originate in America - the hamburger comes from Hamburg, Germany, hence its name.

Go to Scotland and you will find the traditional dish of haggis - a type of round sausage made from sheep's or calf's offal and mixed with oatmeal, suet and seasonings. Traditionally, the sausage was contained in a bag made of the animal's stomach lining, although today an artificial skin is preferable.

Pastas such as spaghetti, macaroni and lasagne are regarded as typical Italian dishes. All pastas are made from a flour paste but their origins are not Italian. Marco Polo, the great Italian traveller, brought this idea from China in the 13th century.

Curry, usually served with rice, is made with meat or vegetables flavoured with spices such as turmeric, coriander and cardamom. Curry is most often associated with Eastern countries such as India and Thailand.

Borsch, a soup made of beetroot and often topped with soured cream, is a favourite Russian dish.

One of the traditional dishes of Mexico is chilli. Usually made with meat and beans flavoured with chilli peppers, it sometimes contains chocolate to add richness. In Europe the best known form of this dish is chilli con carne, which is Spanish for 'chilli with meat'.

Kosher, a Hebrew word meaning 'fit, proper', is a term describing traditional Jewish dishes. There are numerous dietary rules, which concern mainly animal products. For instance, fish must be that which has fins and scales. Meat and milk products may not be cooked or consumed together, or even eaten immediately after one another.

Place a heated dish of melted cheese and white wine or cider in the centre of a table. Dip small pieces of bread or vegetables into it, and you have a fondue. This famous dish of Switzerland is thought to have originated when Swiss peasants had nothing but stale bread and cheese to eat on long winter nights.

In the mid-18th century the British politician John Montague developed the habit of eating beef between slices of toast, to avoid interrupting his long hours of playing cards. Montague was also the 4th Earl of Sandwich, hence the name of his favourite snack.

Measuring Time

The first device used to measure time was a shadow stick. Simply a stick pushed into the ground, it was used once Man realized that the shadow of a tree changes both length and direction as the day progresses.

The primitive shadow stick eventually developed into the more permanent sundial. But the main drawback with a sundial is that it can only be used during the day, when the sun is shining. It cannot be used indoors or on dull days.

One of the earliest devices to measure time without the sun was the water clock, invented by the ancient Egyptians. The clock was basically a bowl with a time scale marked on the side. It would be filled with water, which would trickle out into another bowl. The decreased level of water against the time scale showed how much time had passed.

The first true clock was made by a European monk in the 12th century. It did not have a dial like modern clocks, but simply sounded a bell at certain times. The bell was the call for the monks to go to prayer.

Another ancient clock is the hourglass. It measures only one period of time, and has to be turned over at the end of that period. Long ago, hourglasses were made of various sizes to measure different periods of time. Today, tiny hourglasses are sometimes used to time the boiling of an egg.

During the Middle Ages many clocks were invented, but they were all quite bulky as they depended upon weights as their source of power. It was not until the end of the 15th century, when the coiled spring was invented, that smaller clocks were made.

Until the 18th century clocks were not particularly accurate. This did not matter too much to most people, but to sailors accurate timekeeping was vital for navigation. So, in 1714, the British government offered a prize for a clock that would remain accurate for the duration of a return voyage to the West Indies.

For seven years John Harrison, a skilled clockmaker, worked on the problem. Eventually he produced his 'Number One Chronometer', The Admiralty tested the clock but it did not reach the standard they wanted. They paid Harrison a fee and asked him to try again. In 1761 his 'Number Four Chronometer' was tested, It proved to be so accurate that the Admiralty thought the results were a fluke, and would not pay out any prize money. Three years later Harrison tried again, and this time his clock was even more accurate! Reluctantly the Admiralty paid out half the prize money. Harrison later received the rest of the money, but only after he had sent a petition to the King.

The first pendulum weight-driven clock was made by the Dutch scientist Christiaan Huygens in 1657.

In 1581 the Italian scientist Galileo observed a lamp swinging in Pisa Cathedral. He noticed that it always took the same time to complete a swing. He gave the matter some thought, and realised that a swinging pendulum could be used to time a person's pulse. He also designed a clock using a pendulum, although it was never actually produced.

Candles, with marks representing time intervals, were also used as clocks in days gone by.

Watches, which are simply small clocks, were first made in Germany in the 16th century. Early watches were extremely large and rather unreliable. But as the art of watchmaking developed, they were greatly improved and many were elaborately decorated.

In 1970 the first quartz-crystal watches became available. These contain a tiny piece of quartz that vibrates more than 32,000 times a second. The vibrations control a geared wheel that moves the hands of the watch or operates a digital display.

The World of Stamps

Jean-Baptiste Constant Moâns, the first known stamp dealer, began selling stamps at his bookshop in Brussels in 1855.

The first triangular stamp was issued by the Cape of Good Hope in 1853.

Stamp collecting is probably the most popular hobby in the world and it does not cost any money to start off a simple collection. The formal term for stamp collecting is 'philately', which derives from the Greek language and means 'the love of being tax free'. This definition refers to the fact that, before postage stamps came into use, letters were paid for by the receiver.

In 1873, a 12-year-old schoolboy, Vernon Vaughan, found a British Guiana one-cent stamp. It is the only sample known to exist, making it the rarest stamp in the world. It is valued at approximately £500,000!

The idea of perforating stamps was introduced by Henry Archer, an Irish engineer. Great Britain issued the first perforated stamps in 1854.

The ten-centivo and one-boliviano stamps of Bolivia, issued from 1863-66, measured just 8 x 9.5 millimetres (.31 x .37 in).

The first stamp that was not rectangular in shape was issued by Britain in 1847 - it had eight edges. Despite this octagonal shape, the stamp was cut out square from the sheet (stamps became perforated seven years later).

The first adhesive postage stamp was issued by Britain on 6th May 1840. It is known as the Penny Black, because of its price and colour.

On 7th May 1840, John Tomlynson saved a Penny Black stamp he had received that day. He continued to collect stamps for several years and is the first known stamp collector on record.

A world record price for a stamp was set in 1987, when an American two-cent stamp was sold for $1.1 million (over £600,000). The two-cent stamp dates from 1852, and is known as a 'Lady McGill'.

Today stamps come in various shapes and sizes. Geographical outlines are popular but stamps have also been issued in the shape of parrots, water melons and even bananas!

Most people do not enjoy licking stamps, but a man called John Kenmuir must have. On 30th June 1989 he licked 328 stamps, one after the other. And, incredibly, Kenmuir did it in just four minutes!

In 1913 China issued an enormous stamp for express delivery of mail. It measured a gigantic 247.5 x 69.8 millimetres (9.6 x 2.7 in)!

Great Britain is the only country in the world that does not have its name printed on its stamps.

The nation of Bhutan, in central Asia, once issued stamps in the shape of a gramophone record. What is remarkable about these particular stamps is that they can actually be played on a gramophone!

The first pictorial stamps were issued by New South Wales, Australia. They showed various scenes of the former British colony and were nicknamed 'gold diggings'.

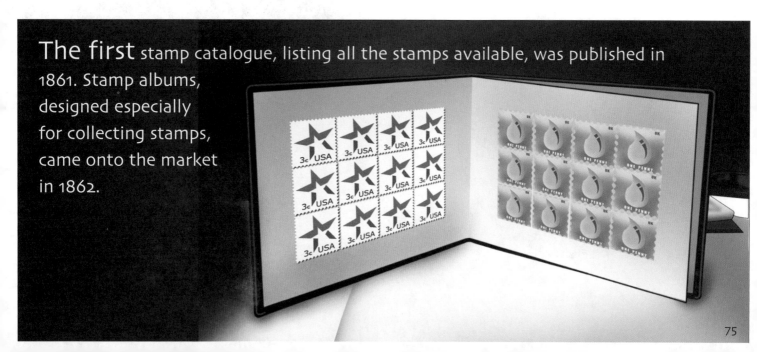

The first stamp catalogue, listing all the stamps available, was published in 1861. Stamp albums, designed especially for collecting stamps, came onto the market in 1862.

Poles Apart

The North Pole and the South Pole are the coldest areas on Earth.

In 1911 two expeditions raced to become the first to reach the South Pole. One expedition was led by Robert Falcon Scott, who had experience of the Antarctic, and the other was led by the Norwegian explorer, Roald Amundsen. It was Amundsen who reached the Pole first. A month later, on 14th December 1911, Scott, who had been dogged by problems throughout his journey, arrived.

The original purpose of Amundsen's expedition was to be the first to reach the North Pole. In 1909, the American explorer Robert Peary claimed to have reached the North Pole, so Amundsen changed his mind and went for the South Pole instead.

The first women to reach the South Pole were Lois Jones, Kay Lindsay, Eileen McSaveney, Jean Pearson, Terry Lee Tickhill and Pam Young. They travelled by aeroplane on 11th November 1969.

South pole

76

Mrs Fran Phillips was the first woman to set foot on the North Pole, on 5th April 1971.

A most unusual journey to the North Pole was made in 1958, when the icy waste was crossed from underneath the ice! Nautilus, an American nuclear submarine commanded by William R. Anderson, made the journey. Nautilus was the world's first nuclear-powered submarine.

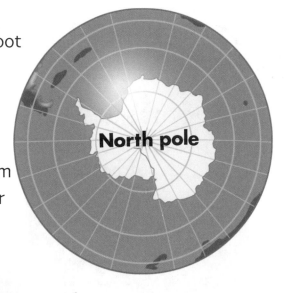

North pole

The area around the North Pole is called the Arctic. The area surrounding the South Pole is the Antarctic.

As Antarctica is at the bottom of the world, it gets very little sun. Heat from the sun that does reach these parts is reflected back by the whiteness of the snow. Therefore the temperature in Antarctica never rises above -15°C, and in the winter months it drops down to an unbearable -64°C!

Voyages of Exploration

On 20th September 1519, Ferdinand Magellan (a Portuguese navigator working for Spain) set sail from Europe with five ships. They reached Rio de la Plata, along the eastern coast of South America, early in 1520. The expedition then travelled southward, looking for a strait which might lead to the Pacific Ocean.

The strait named after Magellan was discovered in 1520. Sadly, Magellan himself was later killed in the Philippines during a battle with the natives. Only one of his five ships completed the trip. The Victoria, ladened with goods from the Far East, struggled into St. Lucar, Spain, on 7th September 1522. Of the 265 men who had set sail three years before, only 17 survived.

Matthew Flinders

(1774-1818) was the last of the great European navigators to explore the coast of Australia. Until his voyages no-one had realised that they were exploring one great land mass, which Flinders himself named 'Australia'.

Although some ships had made landings along the coast of Australia in the years before, the first planned voyages to Australia were those of the Dutch explorer Abel Janszoon Tasman, from 1642 to 1644. He discovered several stretches of the north coast and the southern part of what he called Van Diemen's Land. This is now known as Tasmania in honour of the man who discovered it.

The next major Australian exploration was made by Captain James Cook in 1770. Cook, considered the greatest explorer of the 18th century, was the first to approach Australia from the East, exploring areas that had yet to be discovered by Europeans. He made three voyages to the region and charted much of the shores of New Zealand and Australia.

Vasco da Gama, the Portuguese explorer, was the first man to sail from Europe to India and back (Bartholomew Diaz had sailed around the Cape of Good Hope in 1488, but soon turned back as his men were complaining about the voyage!). Da Gama sailed from Portugal in July 1497, and reached India the following May. When he returned to Portugal his ships were filled with spices.

Amerigo Vespucci, after whom America is named, explored the South American coast from 1500 to 1502. Until then, in spite of the journeys of Columbus, the continents of North and South America had been unknown in Europe.

Like Colombus before him, Ferdinand Magellan wanted to find a westward sea route to Asia. Thanks to the discoveries of Columbus and Amerigo Vespucci, the existence of the American continents was now known.

One of the most famous explorers of all time was Christopher Columbus. In 1492 he set sail from Spain hoping to find a westerly sea route to the riches and spices of Asia. He reached the Caribbean Islands but was convinced that he had landed in Asia. He maintained this belief even after making three subsequent voyages to the region.

Down to the Sea in Ships

A log floating downriver was probably the first 'boat' known to man. Unfortunately, as a floating log only moves with the flow of the water, people had to use their hands as paddles. Man soon discovered wooden paddles were much better at moving the boat along. Later the logs were hollowed out and simple sails were fitted.

The ancient Egyptians and Romans and, later, the Vikings, used large ships powered by sails and by several men rowing with oars. To show off their manliness the Viking seamen would run around the outside of the ship - on the oars! As the rowing did not stop while they were running, they had to be quick and nimble to avoid falling into the water.

It is said that the first person to suggest steam power for ships was a Frenchman, Salomon de Caus, in 1615. Another Frenchman, Denys Papin, claimed to have powered a boat by steam engine in 1707. The vessel was apparently tested on the River Fulda in Germany, but as it was smashed by local boatmen who thought it would deprive them of their livelihood, there is no actual evidence that the boat existed.

In 1772 Le Comte Joseph d'Auxiron and Le Chevalier Charles Monnin de Eollenai launched a steamboat on the River Seine. They then spent several months installing paddle wheels and the engine. The day after work was completed, they planned to take the vessel on her maiden voyage. Unfortunately the weight of the engine was too great and the boat sank!

The Mayflower was a 180-tonne vessel that crossed the Atlantic in 1620. On board were 102 passengers heading for America to start a new life. One quarter of the passengers were Separatist Puritans, later known as 'Pilgrims'.

The 18th century saw the introduction of East Indiamen. These powerful merchant ships were designed to carry the tea harvest from China to Europe as quickly as possible. The most famous of these ships is the Cutty Sark, built in 1869, which can still be seen at Greenwich, London.

The first successful steamboat was a paddle vessel designed by an American, John Fitch. The boat was launched in 1787 on the Delaware River, Philadelphia. Thirteen years later Fitch established the world's first steamboat passenger service.

Other pioneers tried steam power but the first practical steam-powered vessel was the Charlotte Dundas. This was built by William Symington in 1802, and was the first vessel equipped with a crankshaft between the piston and paddle wheel.

Travelling by Train

The first railways date back to the 16th century: horse-drawn wagons with wooden wheels running on wooden rails were used in British and western European coal mines.

The first person to apply steam power to the mine railways was Richard Trevithick, a Cornish engineer. His steam-powered train made its debut on 11th February 1804, at the Pen-y-Darren ironworks in Wales.

Trevithick believed that his steam engine could be used to power passenger trains. To prove his point he set up a circular track in London in 1808, near what is now Euston Station. People were given a ride for one shilling (5p). The name of the engine used for this venture was Catch-me-who-can.

Although several steam engines had been invented before it, the Puffing Billy was the first true railway engine. It was built by William Hedley for use at a colliery in 1813.

In the USA, railways are called 'railroads'. The first track to cross the USA was completed on 10th May 1869. It was the joint development of two companies: Union-Pacific Railway and the Central Pacific Company. By 1930, the USA had almost 430,000 miles of track!

The first iron railway track was laid at Coalbrookdale, England, in 1760.

An Englishman, William Wilkinson, was the first to build a railway in France. He built a line for a factory in Indret in 1778. It was not until 1828, however, that the first French passenger service began.

The town of La Cima, Peru, boasts the highest railway in the world - it gradually climbs to a height of 4783 metres (15,693 ft). La Cima also boasts the world's highest railway junction and the world's highest railway tunnel. It has been in service for over 100 years.

In November 1994 passenger services began from London to Paris via the Channel Tunnel. The 'Chunnel' is actually three tunnels bored beneath the English Channel. It was on 1st December 1990, after two years of drilling, that French and English crews met for the first time in one of the tunnels.

Russia's Trans-Siberian Railway, completed in 1916, runs from Chelyabinsk in the Ural Mountains to Nakhoda. Connections to Moscow and extensions to Vladivostock on the Pacific coast, make it the longest railway in the world - the entire journey of some 9,250 kilometres (5,750 miles) takes over eight days to complete.

Grand Central in New York is the largest railway station in the world. Every day over 500 trains use the station.

The first passenger-carrying railway, the Stockton & Darlington line, opened in 1825. The line used the Locomotion No. 1, a steam engine invented by George Stephenson. Another famous Stephenson engine was the Rocket, which he built in 1829 for the Liverpool and Manchester Railway.

On the opening day of the Liverpool and Manchester Railway, 15th September 1830, tragedy struck. The Member of Parliament for Liverpool, William Huskisson, was run over by Stephenson's Rocket. His thigh was fractured, and he later died - the first fatal accident in the history of railways.

Cars from the Past

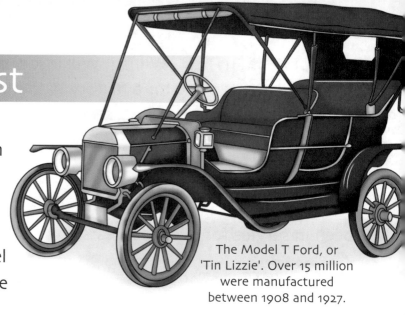

Henry Ford was the first person to make cars in great numbers. He built his first car in 1896 and in 1903 founded the Ford Motor company. The first car produced was the Model T, in 1908. By 1919, one half of all the world's cars were Model T Fords!

The Model T Ford, or 'Tin Lizzie'. Over 15 million were manufactured between 1908 and 1927.

The first mechanically powered vehicle to be used on roads was the steam carriage, invented by Nicholas Cugnot, a French artillery officer. In 1763 he built a model of the carriage and after 6 years of development he constructed a full-size carriage. It had a top speed of 3.6 kilometres (2.25 miles) per hour and had to stop every 15 minutes for a new supply of steam. The carriage was very successful and the French government ordered one to be made for the Royal Arsenal in Paris. During tests, however, this machine crashed into a wall and was deemed too dangerous for military service.

Richard Trevithick, a Cornish engineer, designed a steam carriage in 1801. The first time he took friends for a ride was the first time that passengers had ever travelled in a powered vehicle. But when they stopped at an inn, they forgot to put out the fire. The boiler burned dry and the carriage burst into flames!

Karl Benz built his first car in 1885, but it did not last long - he crashed it into a wall. Two years later Benz showed an improved model at the Paris Exhibition.

Mercedes Jellinek, an 11-year-old girl, gave her name to the Daimler Mercedes, which was built in 1901. She was the daughter of racing driver Emile Jellinek, who suggested the name.

The Volkswagen was originally designed by Ferdinand Porsche in the 1930s. Production began in 1938 at the request of the German dictator Adolf Hitler, who wanted every German citizen to own a car ('Volkswagen' means 'people's car'). One model was the famous Beetle, which became the most popular car in the world.

The original Volkswagon Beetle was discontinued in 1978. Over 19 million cars had been sold.

THE FIRST

The first time a radio was fitted in a car was in August 1921, at the suggestion of the Cardiff and South Wales Wireless Society.

The first car fitted with a reversing light was the Wills-Sainte Claire, an American automobile built in 1921.

The first modern motorway, opened in 1924, was built between Milan and Varese, Italy.

The makers of the Pan, an American car of 1921, had a novel idea - the seats in the car could be made up into a bed.

A German salesmen, Nikolaus Otto, improved the Lenoir engine and used coal gas as fuel. His engineer, Gottleib Daimler, suggested using petrol vapour. Daimler left Otto and built the first petrol-powered motorcycle. He then started to build cars, and the name Daimler soon became famous the world over.

The first vehicle to be powered by a petrol engine was designed by Siegfried Marcus in 1875. The engine was similar to one designed about 15 years earlier by the French engineer Jean-Joseph Lenoir. Marcus drove his vehicle through the streets of Vienna, but was stopped by the police because they considered it too noisy.

Another pioneering development of the motor car industry was the Mini, designed by Sir Alec Issigonis. It came onto the market in 1959 and was an instant success.

Mini, Britain's most recognizable automobile.

The Story of the Bicycle

Possibly the most important invention in the story of the bicycle was the pneumatic tyre. A veterinary surgeon, J.B. Dunlop, invented a pneumatic tyre for his son's bicycle. It was an immediate success and within seven years the solid tyre had almost disappeared.

In 1970-71 Dennis Wickham rode from London to Brisbane, Australia, on a penny-farthing. The journey of 24,000 kilometres (14,900 miles) took 19 months to complete.

High-wheeled bikes were difficult to ride, so inventors tried reducing the size of the front wheel to make the machine more stable. In 1879 H.J. Lawson designed his 'bicyclette', with both wheels of almost the same size. This was the first bicycle to be powered by a chain drive to the rear wheel.

The first pedal-driven bicycle was invented by Kirkpatric Macmillan, a Scottish blacksmith, in 1839. The pedals were attached to cranks which drove the rear wheel. It was an ingenious machine for its time, but was not particularly popular.

James Starley, 'the father of the cycle industry', developed a most unusual bicycle in 1871. Called the Ariel, it had a large front wheel which enabled the rider to cover a greater distance for each turn of the pedals. Similar designs soon followed and were known as 'ordinaries', which became better known by the nickname of penny-farthings.

The first practical tandem was designed by A.J. Wilson and Dan Albone in 1886. It had dual steering control, which must have caused a few arguments between the two riders!

In 1963 Alex Moulton introduced the Moulton Mini. The wheels were just 40 centimetres (16 in) in diameter, and it had a rubber suspension system to ensure a smooth ride.

The people of Paris had quite a shock in 1791: the Comte de Sivrac rode a wooden horse on wheels through the gardens of the Palais-Royal. It was propelled by striding along the ground with an exaggerated walking action.

In 1861 a French coach repairer fitted pedals to the front wheels of his hobby horse and called it velocipede. In England, though, it was nicknamed the boneshaker, because of the rough ride it offered!

After the 'bicyclette' came several similar designs. Known as 'safeties', the most popular was the Rover Safety produced in 1885 by J.K. Stanley, the nephew of James Stanley, who designed the Ariel.

In a church in Stoke Poges, Buckinghamshire, there is a stained-glass window which depicts a bicycle-like vehicle. The window was made in 1642, over 100 years before the first recorded use of such a vehicle.

In 1817 Baron Karl von Drais de Sauerbrun startled the people of Manheim, Germany, with his draisienne. It had a steerable front wheel, a cushioned saddle and an arm rest. The draisienne became very popular; in England it was known as a swiftwalker or a dandy horse.

The Computer Age

Today computers are everywhere. We use them at school, in offices and even at home. Yet the electronic computer as we know it is a relatively new invention.

Today some computers are so small they can fit in your pocket!

The world's first computers were extremely large and very expensive. Companies that installed computers often had to build special rooms for them, with air conditioning to keep the machines cool and false floors to hide the tremendous amount of cables.

The power in early computers was controlled by valves, or electron tubes. These were made of glass, were quite large, became extremely hot during use and required an enormous amount of power. From around 1953 onwards, valves were replaced by transistors, which were more compact and less expensive. Computers could now be made smaller and more powerful.

In the 1960s the 'chip' was developed. Chips are tiny electrical circuits built up in layers on a wafer of silicon, a common element found in rocks and sand. Although readily available, silicon cannot be used for chips until it has been processed to make sure it is flawless. Chips soon replaced transistors as the computer's source of power control. Then the microchips followed, holding the equivalent of millions of transistors.

A microprocessor chip measures only about 50 millimetres (1.95 in) square, and yet it contains more components than the bulky computers of the 1940s and '50s.

The first home computer was the Altair, which became available in 1975.

The compact home computers of today are far more powerful than the enormous machines installed in offices just 40 years ago.

The development of computers is linked closely with Man's race into space. But today, basic home computers are more powerful than those used by the first astronauts!

The first completely electronic computer was built between 1942 and 1946 at the University of Pennsylvania, USA, by J. Presper Eckert and John W. Mauchly. It was called ENIAC, which stands for Electronic Numerical Integrator and Calculator. ENIAC contained 18,000 valves, and used so much electricity that it dimmed the city lights when first switched on.

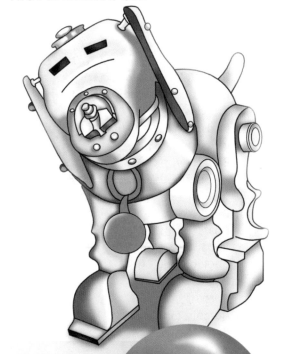

Chips are not only used in computers. They are now found in a variety of products, from watches to sewing machines. Chips are also used in the robots that make the chips!

Index

A

Abominable Snowman (Yeti), 7
Aborigines, 57
Africa, 24
Alsatians, 21
Amundsen, Roald (explorer), 76
Angel Falls (Venezuela), 26
Animals, 10, 11, 19, 20, 21, 24, 25
(see also individual species)
Antarctica, 76, 77
Apples, 37
Arctic, 76, 77
Artemis, the Temple of, 58
Ashurbanipal, King of Syaria, 46
Aurora Australis, 27
Aurora Borealis, 27
Australia, 15, 26, 78
Ayer's Rock (Australia), 26

B

Babylon, 58
Bach, Johann Sebastian (composer), 55
Ballet, 37, 54
Basenjis, 19
Basilisks, 4
Bears, 23
Beethoven, Ludwig van, (composer), 55
Berlioz, Hecto, (composer), 55
Berwick-on-Tweed (Scotland), 37
Bicycles, 86, 87
Birds, 12, 13, 16, 17, 18
Birds' nests, 14, 15
Bladderworts, 33
Bloodhounds, 19
Bluefish, 8
Boadicea, 52
Boats, 80, 81
Bonaparte, Napoleon, 36, 39
Book of Kells, 47
Books, 46-48
Borsch, 71
Borzois, 21
Brachiosaurus, 27
Buff-tip moths, 11
Bull-baiting, 19
Bulldogs, 19
Butterflies, 10, 11

C

Caerphilly Castle, 61
Cars, 80, 81
Castles, 60, 61
Caterpillars, 10
Cat-fish, 9
Cats, 22
Caxton, William, (printer), 48
Centaurs, 5
Chameleons, 10
Channel Tunnel, 83
Chihuahuas, 19
Chimeras, 5
China, 24, 46, 47
Chopin, Frederic François, (composer), 55
Chow chows, 21
Clocks, 72, 73
Clothes, 68, 69
Coelacanths, 9
Collies, 21
Colossus of Rhodes, 59
Columbus, Christopher (explorer), 79
Composers, 54, 55
Compsognathus, 28
Computers, 88, 89
Cook, Captain James, (navigator), 78
Crabs, 11
Crocket, Davy, (frontiersman), 51
Curry, 67
Cutty Sark, 81

D

Dachshunds, 20
Dead-leaf moths, 11
Decorator crab, 11
Dicken Medal, 22
Dinosaurs, 28-30
(see also individual species)
Diplodocus, 29
Dogs, 19-21, 23, 39
(see also individual species)
Dover Castle, 60
Dragons, 4

E

Edward I, King, 60
Egypt, 4, 47, 58, 80
Eiffel Tower, 420
Electric rays, 9

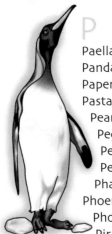

Contents

500

Questions
&Answers

The Human Body

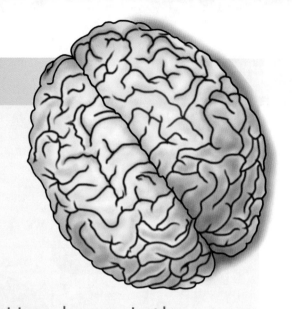

What are goose pimples?

Goose pimples are little bumps that appear on our skin when we are cold. The cold air causes muscles at the base of hairs on the skin to stiffen, resulting in these small bumps. The hairs stand up, trapping air between them and giving the body some insulation against the cold.

What makes body hair stand on end?

When you are frightened you may feel a tingling sensation down the back of your neck. This is your hair standing on end! It is caused by small muscles at the root of each hair. Although it is not very visible in humans you can see it clearly when a cat is frightened. Its hairs stand erect so the animal appears bigger to its enemies.

How heavy is the human brain?

For men, the average weight is just over 1.36 kilograms (3 lb). Womens' brains are about 1.25 kilograms (2 lb 12 oz).

Which is our largest muscle?

The largest muscle is the buttock muscle, which you use to lift your legs. It is called the gluteus maximus.

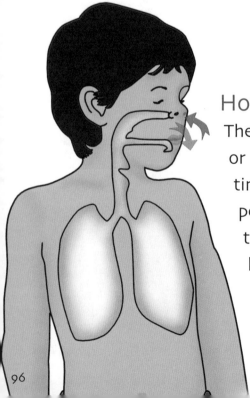

How often do we breathe?

The rate at which a person breathes varies according to his or her age. A newborn baby breathes in and out about 65 times a minute. By the age of 15, the number of breaths per minute decreases to about 20. As a person gets older, the rate decreases further. By the age of 40 he or she is breathing approximately 18 times a minute. These figures vary according to health, level of fitness and whether or not one is standing still or is active at the time.

Which muscle has the longest name?

Just curl your upper lip and you'll be using the human muscle with the longest name: the levator labii superioris aleoquae nasi.

What causes a heart attack?

Blood is carried to the heart by the arteries. If an artery gets blocked, the blood cannot get through and the heart cannot function properly. As a result, the heart is damaged, causing a heart attack. The arteries get blocked due to a variety of health factors.

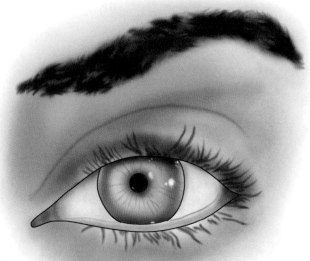

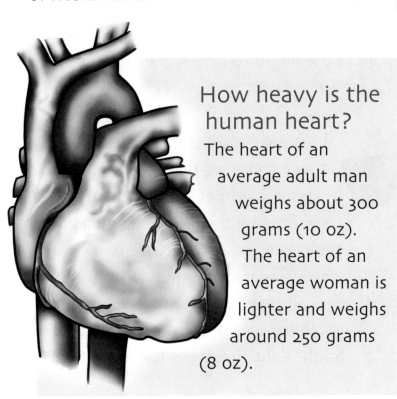

How heavy is the human heart?

The heart of an average adult man weighs about 300 grams (10 oz). The heart of an average woman is lighter and weighs around 250 grams (8 oz).

Why do we have eyebrows?

Although we have hair all over our bodies, it tends to grow thickest where some form of protection is needed. Both eyebrows and eyelashes are designed to protect the eyes from dust.

How many teeth do we have?

Unfortunately, not many people have a full set of teeth. They decay or have to be taken out because we eat too many sweet things or do not look after them properly. However, a full set in an adult would consist of 32 teeth.

Which is our smallest muscle?

The smallest muscle in the human body is attached to the smallest bone. Called the stapedius, it controls the stirrup bone and is only 0.127 centimetre (1/16 in) long.

Why do skin types vary?

The colour of a person's skin depends upon the amount of melanin it contains. Melanin is a brown substance present in everyone's skin. Ultra-violet rays in sunlight cause the skin to produce more melanin and this is why people in hot climates have a darker skin than those who live in cooler areas of the world. The purpose of the melanin, which is deposited on the outer layers of the skin, is to protect the skin from the sun.

What is the purpose of a yawn?

One usually yawns when bored or tired. Yawning makes you draw in breath, filling your lungs with air. This increases the oxygen supply to the blood to help wake yourself up.

Why do people blink?

Every time we blink, normally about six times a minute, a tear is secreted by the lachrymal gland in the corner of the eye. This tear spreads over the cornea to keep the eyeball clean and moist. The amount you blink increases when wind, dust or bright light threatens to harm the eye.

What is a wart?

It is a growth on the skin that is caused by a virus. Although unsightly, warts are usually painless. They should only be removed by a doctor who will either freeze or burn them off with acid.

Can you get warts from toads?

Many people believe that you can get warts from toads because the toad's skin is covered with bumps. But it is just superstition - you cannot get warts from toads.

What is a stitch?

A stitch is a pain felt on either side of the body, usually after severe exertion. It is caused when normally inactive muscles tighten and press against the nerves. In a healthy person, a stitch is nothing to worry about and soon passes.

What is the longest bone?

Well, it is not the spine for that is made up of several bones. The longest bone in the human body is the thigh bone, or femur.

How many bones do you have?

It depends upon how old you are. Young people have more bones than adults. As a person grows up, some bones separate and increase the number, while other bones fuse to reduce the number. By the time a person reaches full adulthood, there are normally 206 bones in the body.

What is the shortest bone?

The shortest bone is the stirrup. It is in the inner ear. It is so called because it is the same shape as a stirrup used on a saddle.

Why do people get wrinkles?

As a person gets older the body fat is renewed less readily. Because of this, the skin has a smaller area to cover and so it wrinkles up.

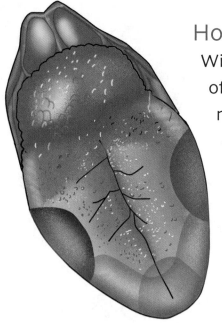

How do we taste food?

With our taste buds. The tongue is covered with about 3,000 of them. When they are stimulated, the taste buds send messages to the brain. These messages are interpreted as different tastes according to where the taste bud is located on the tongue. The tip of the tongue, for example, is particularly sensitive to salty or sweet foods; the back discerns bitter tastes; and the sides respond to anything sour. Our perception of taste is also affected by the smell, appearance and the texture of food.

What is a bruise?

Bruises are caused by the rupturing of blood vessels under the skin. Gradually, the blood decomposes and is absorbed. As this happens, the blood loses oxygen and turns blue. Later, it changes to green and yellow until it eventually disappears altogether.

What is the normal temperature of the human body?

The average normal body temperature is 36.9°C (98.4°F). Body temperature is a general indication of good or bad health, which is why doctors often take patients' temperatures.

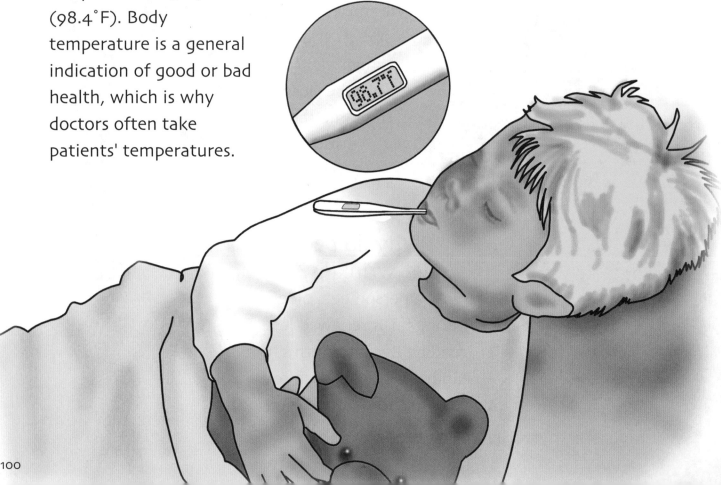

What is an element?

All matter consists of elements. An element is a substance that cannot be broken down into anything simpler. This particular definition was given by the chemist Robert Boyle in the 17th century and it still holds true today.

How many elements are there?

There are 94 natural elements: two are liquids, 11 are gases and 81 are solids.

Who invented the Bunsen burner?

Robert Wilhelm Bunsen, a German professor of chemistry, developed the Bunsen burner in 1855. It is a widely used gas burner that consists of an adjustable air valve attached to the base of a metal tube.

How does a barometer work?

There are two main types of barometer - mercury and aneroid. The mercury barometer houses a glass tube containing mercury. The height of the column of mercury in the tube is controlled by air pressure on the mercury. When the atmospheric pressure falls (an indication of forthcoming wind or rain), the pressure on the mercury is decreased and some of it runs out from the base of the tube into a special container. When the pressure rises (indicating fair weather), the mercury is forced back up into the tube. In most barometers, the tube of mercury is hidden and its movements operate a dial on the front of the barometer. Aneroid barometers work on a different principle. Inside the aneroid barometer is a small metal box with a thin lid. Most of the air has been withdrawn from the box so it contains springs which prevent the box from being crushed by the air pressure. The lid of the box is moved up and down by the air pressure and this movement is monitored by a lever that makes the pointer move across the dial on the front of the barometer.

How does an aerosol work?

When it was first invented in 1942, the aerosol was called the 'bug bomb' because it contained insecticide for use by American military forces. Today, under its modern name of 'aerosol', the bug bomb has a thousand and one different uses - from making air smell fresher to cleaning ovens and from producing whipped cream to spraying on bandages. The modern aerosol is made of a tube of tin-plate or glass, at the top of which is a plastic plunger and valve. Leading from the valve is a dip tube through which the contents are propelled. With the product, there is a liquid which turns to gas at room temperature. Pressure exerted by the gas pushes the contents of the dip tube up and out through the nozzle when the plunger is pressed.

What is the Beaufort scale?

Admiral Sir Francis Beaufort devised the Beaufort Scale in 1806. It is used to record wind speed. The Beaufort Scale categorises wind speed on a scale of 0 to 12, 0 being calm weather and 12 a hurricane.

Which gases are found in air?

Air is a mixture of gases, the main ones being oxygen and nitrogen. There are also small amounts of carbon dioxide, argon, neon, helium, xenon and krypton.

How does a Bunsen burner work?

When oxygen is combined with gas, the gas burns with a greater heat. The Bunsen burner has a metal collar at its base which can be turned to expose holes in the main cylinder. When these holes are open, oxygen is drawn in and the flame burns with a greater intensity. Strangely, not all parts of the flame have the same temperature. The brightest part, in the middle of the flame, burns at about 300°C (527°F). The hottest part of the flame is at the top, where it is almost invisible, and has a temperature of about 1,550°C (2,822°F).

How was the sundial invented?

The sundial was probably devised by people who noticed that shadows change length and direction during the day. As a result, early man developed the shadow stick, which over a period of time was developed into the sundial.

How does a vacuum flask work?

A vacuum flask consists of a glass or metal bottle with double walls from which the air has been removed. Heat cannot travel through a vacuum but it is possible for some heat to radiate from one wall to the other. This is why the innermost wall is silvered - so that the heat is reflected back into the bottle.

How does a kaleidoscope work?

Inside the tube of a kaleidoscope there are two or three mirrors positioned at an angle of 60° to each other. Placed between the mirrors are pieces of coloured paper or plastic. What the viewer sees, as well as the pieces of plastic or paper, are their reflections in the mirrors. These images can form a colourful pattern which is changed by shaking the kaleidoscope or by revolving the end section of the tube.

What is an Archimedean screw?

It is an ancient means of raising water from a river or ditch. It consists of a long tube with a large screw fitted inside. When one end of the screw is placed in the water and the handle is turned, water rises through the tube and comes out of the top. Although it is named after the Greek inventor Archimedes, it is quite likely that this device, or something similar, was around long before he was born.

Does the Archimedean screw have other uses?

Yes, and you might even have one in your kitchen. If you look at a food mincer, you will find that it also consists of a large screw within a tube. When the handle is turned, or the electricity switched on, the food is forced along the screw and through the tube. At the front end of the mincer is a metal grill with a perforated disc attached. The food is forced through the holes in the disc and is minced.

Medicine

What are antibiotics?

Antibiotics are chemicals produced by a micro-organism that can stop bacteria growth or destroy other bacteria. Their development has revolutionised the treatment of disease.

When were X-rays discovered?

In 1895, the German scientist Wilhelm Van Roentgen was studying the behaviour of electricity in a vacuum tube (one end of which was coated with fluorescent salts). After one experiment, he found that a nearby photographic plate looked as if it had been exposed - even though it was covered. Van Roentgen concluded that some form of 'invisible rays' had come from the tube and affected the plate. He named them X-rays, as so little was known about them. Further research found these rays could pass through materials such as cardboard and wood, but were stopped by materials like lead and bone. The scientist quickly realised that X-rays would have great medical use and today every large hospital has an X-ray department.

What is a stethoscope?

It is an instrument used by physicians to listen to sounds emitted from various organs, particularly the lungs.

Who invented the stethoscope?

The stethoscope was invented in 1814 by a French doctor, René Theophile Laennec. Early stethoscopes consisted of a wooden tube about 30 centimetres (12 in) long.

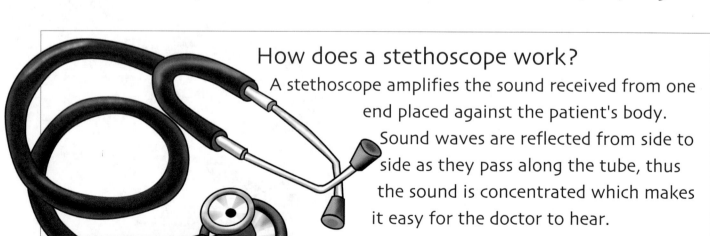

How does a stethoscope work?

A stethoscope amplifies the sound received from one end placed against the patient's body. Sound waves are reflected from side to side as they pass along the tube, thus the sound is concentrated which makes it easy for the doctor to hear.

What was the 'Black Death'?

The Black Death is a name given to the bubonic plague that spread from Asia to Europe in the 14th century. The disease was carried by fleas on infected rats which were found on ships traveling from the Far East. It is estimated the disease killed between 25 and 50 per cent of the European population.

What is a placebo?

A placebo is a harmless drug or pill. Placebos are given to people who think they are ill when really they are not. They are also used as a controlled substance in medical tests.

What is acupuncture?

Acupuncture is the ancient Chinese practice of curing certain ailments by pricking the skin with long needles. Very often the needles are inserted well away from the affected part of the body. This is because there are thought to be special channels, called meridians, flowing through the body and each meridian serves a particular organ.

Why is the village of Oberammergau famous?

In the 17th century, the village of Oberammergau in the Bavarian Alps was afflicted by the bubonic plague. As more and more people died, the elders called all the villagers to church, and they agreed to devote one year in every ten to the presentation of a play, called the Passion Play, dramatising the death and resurrection of Jesus Christ. After that promise, there were no more deaths from the plague and, with the exception of the war years, the play has been performed every ten years since 1634. The whole village takes part and people flock from all over the world to watch.

Who invented acupuncture?

It was Emperor Fu Shi, who lived some 5,000 years ago in China. He believed everything was a balance of two forces: Yin and Yang. Fu Shi also thought the forces to be in the human body, remaining in balance unless illness struck. The purpose of acupuncture is to restore this balance.

Our Planet and Beyond

What is a comet?

There are three parts to a comet: the nucleus, or head, which is made up of ice and particles of debris; the coma, gases that surround the nucleus; and the tail, which is composed of small dust-like particles and may be millions of kilometres in length. Comets travel around the sun, approaching it head first and leaving it tail first.

What is the largest meteorite ever found?

The largest known meteorite still lies where it fell to Earth at Grootfontein in South Africa. Discovered in 1920, it measures 2.75 metres (9 ft) by 2.43 metres (8 ft) and is estimated to weigh about 58 tonnes (59 tons).

What caused a large crater in Siberia?

In 1908 a large asteroid, believed to be the size of a football pitch, exploded 8 kilometres (5 miles) above Siberia. It shattered some 1800 kilometres squared (695 sq. miles) of trees and set fire to the clothes of people over 400 kilometres (248 miles) away. The shock waves were felt as far away as London.

What is the greenhouse effect?

The Earth is warmed by the sun. Some of the heat is then given out by the planet in the form of infra-red radiation. Normally this would disappear into space, but gases we produce (like petrol fumes) have created an invisible barrier around our atmosphere and some of the infra-red heat cannot get through it. As a result the heat stays in our atmosphere and, according to some scientists, is making our planet permanently warmer. It is thought this will eventually lead to a change in the Earth's climate, possibly causing the polar regions to melt!

What is a meteor?

Meteors are small particles or fragments of comets that burn up as they enter the Earth's atmosphere. They can be seen in the night sky and are often called shooting stars.

What is a meteorite?

A meteorite is a chunk of iron or rock which falls to Earth from space. Because they are much bigger than meteors, meteorites do not burn up completely when they enter the Earth's atmosphere. They vary in size and weight.

What are black holes?

The largest stars in the universe (much bigger than our own sun) do not die out over a period of millions of years like those of a smaller mass - they end their lives in an immense nuclear explosion. Known as 'supernovae', they occur when the gravity of the star becomes so great that it 'collapses' in on itself. However, with some stars the gravity is so powerful that it goes on collapsing endlessly, crushing the matter within it. The density of this body goes on increasing and the force of gravity keeps rising until absolutely nothing can escape - not even light - resulting in a 'black hole'. Anything that falls within this object's gravity-pull cannot escape. Although they are invisible, black holes can be detected by X-ray satellites and the first known black hole was detected in the constellation Cygnus in 1972.

Why is the sea blue?

There are several factors that affect the colour of the sea. On a bright summer day, the sea usually appears blue because it reflects the colour of the sky. If the day is overcast, then the sea appears to be black or grey. If you are near the shore, the sea bed will also influence the colour you see. The amount of salt in the water is another influence - the saltier the water the more blue the sea.

What is the longest river?

The Nile River of north-eastern Africa reaches a length of 6,670 kilometres (4,145 miles).

Which is the deepest lake?

It is Lake Baikal in Siberia, which reaches a depth of over 1,700 metres (5,577 ft). As the lake is so deep it also holds the most water, even more than Lake Superior.

What is the highest waterfall?

It is Angel Falls in Venezuela, South America. It measures almost 1,000 metres (3,000 ft) in height.

Which is the biggest lake in the world?

Lake Superior, one of the Great Lakes of North America, is the largest freshwater lake in the world. It covers more than 83,000 square kilometres (some 32,000 sq. miles), and about 200 different rivers flow into it.

What is a tsunami?

A tsunami is a gigantic sea wave common in the Pacific Ocean. Special warning systems have been set up to warn fisherman and sailors when a tsunami is approaching.

What shape is a snowflake?
The amazing thing about snowflakes is that every one is a different shape! All snowflakes are six-sided and formed of intricate patterns, but they are all different.

What is the highest mountain in Britain?
Ben Nevis, in the highlands region of Scotland, reaches a height of 1,343 metres (4,406 ft).

Which volcano has the biggest crater?
Mount Aso in Japan has a circumference of 114 kilometres (71 miles), and it measures 27 kilometres (17 miles) from north to south and 16 kilometres (10 miles) from east to west.

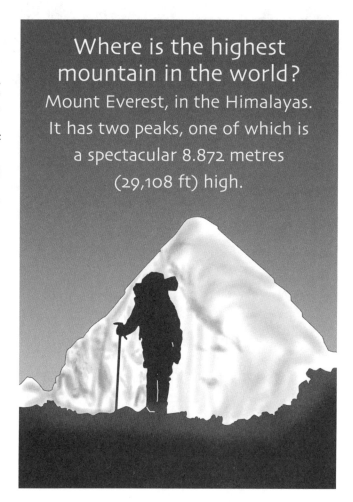

Where is the highest mountain in the world?
Mount Everest, in the Himalayas. It has two peaks, one of which is a spectacular 8.872 metres (29,108 ft) high.

Where is the highest volcano?
Cerro Aconcagua in Argentina, with a height of 6,960 metres (22,834 ft), is the highest extinct volcano in the world. Of the dormant volcanoes, Volcan Llullaillaco, on the border of Argentina and Chile, is the highest at 6,723 metres (22,057 ft). Argentina also has the highest active volcano, Volcan Antofalla, which is 6,450 metres (21,161 ft) high.

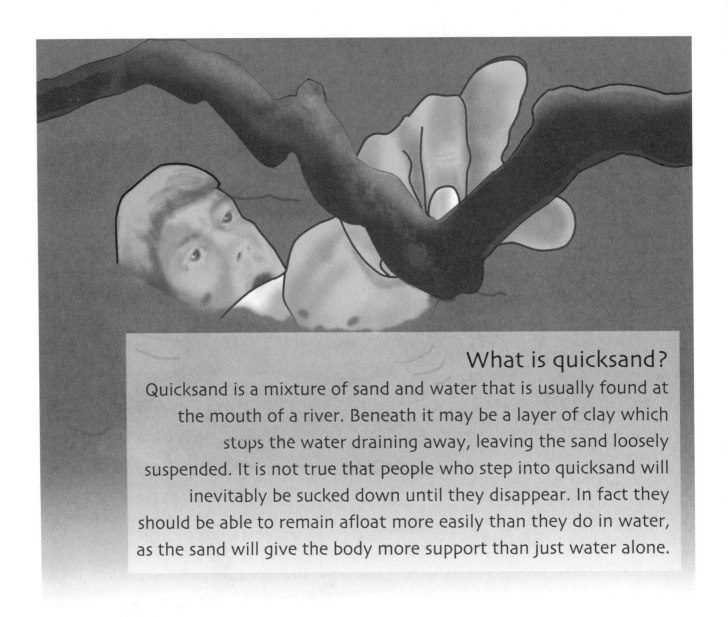

What is quicksand?

Quicksand is a mixture of sand and water that is usually found at the mouth of a river. Beneath it may be a layer of clay which stops the water draining away, leaving the sand loosely suspended. It is not true that people who step into quicksand will inevitably be sucked down until they disappear. In fact they should be able to remain afloat more easily than they do in water, as the sand will give the body more support than just water alone.

What are Singing Sands?

There are over 100 sandy areas of the world that give out musical notes or eerie squeals when someone walks over them. The sounds vary, as do the explanations for their occurrence. In Afghanistan, it is believed the drum-like noises in the sands of Reg Ruwan are caused by ghostly horsemen shoeing their horses in an underground cave. The noises heard on a beach in Hawaii are said to be the cries of the dead, although some people say the sounds are more like the baying of hounds. There are also singing sands in the British Isles, some of the most famous are at Studland Bay in Dorset, Bamburgh in Northumberland, Forth Oer in North Wales and Eigg in the Hebrides. The reason for the noises has never been satisfactorily explained. It is, however, generally accepted that as someone walks over sand, any sounds are the result of air rushing in to fill tiny spaces between the grains.

What is the legend of Lorelei?

The legend of Lorelei tells of a young German girl who drowned herself in the River Rhine, because her lover had been unfaithful to her. She became a temptress and sat on the rocks combing her long hair and singing. Passing sailors were so enraptured by her they forgot to look where they were going, and their boats were dashed against the rock that now bears her name.

Who holds the world on his shoulders?

Greek mythology states that a race of giants called the Titans once ruled the world. When they were conquered by the god Zeus, a giant called Atlas was condemned to hold the world on his shoulders.

Why do we blow out birthday candles?

When you blow out the candles on a birthday cake you are following a custom created by the ancient Greeks. On the sixth day of each month, the birthday of Artemis (goddess of the hunt), the ancient Greeks made a honey cake topped with burning candles in her honour. As each candle was extinguished, the people prayed to the goddess for a present. In the same way, a person who blows out all the candles on a birthday cake, it is believed, will have a wish granted.

Who was Cupid?

Cupid was the Roman god of love. His equivalent in Greek mythology was Eros.

What was Atlantis?

According to legend, Atlantis was a beautiful city that sank beneath the sea. For many centuries people have tried to confirm if the story is true or not. Remains of ancient cities have been found under the sea but whether or not any were part of Atlantis is unknown.

Weather

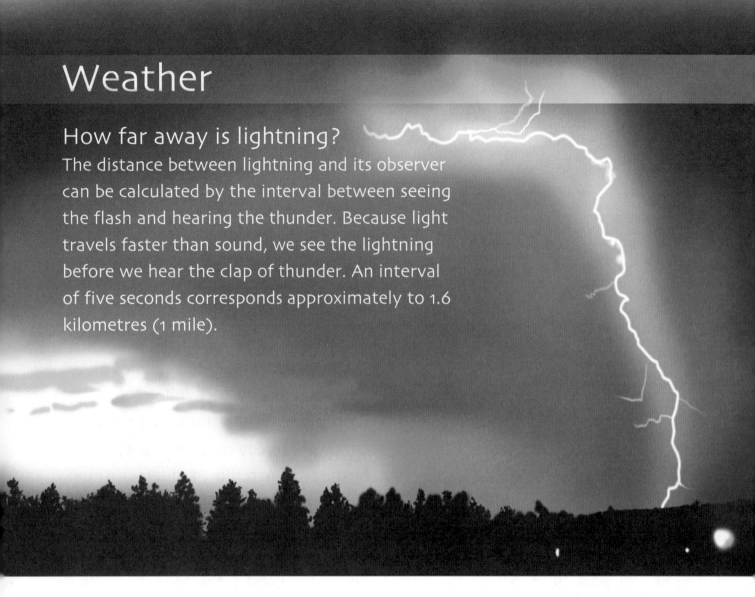

How far away is lightning?

The distance between lightning and its observer can be calculated by the interval between seeing the flash and hearing the thunder. Because light travels faster than sound, we see the lightning before we hear the clap of thunder. An interval of five seconds corresponds approximately to 1.6 kilometres (1 mile).

What causes lightning?

Lightning is simply a large electrical spark. It is caused by electric charges jumping from one cloud to another, or from a cloud to the Earth. This occurs because different positive and negative charges are created between clouds, or between clouds and the ground, during a storm. When the difference becomes too great, a discharge of electricity occurs, resulting in a gigantic flash.

Why does milk sour in a thunderstrom?

Micro-organisms called bacteria lactis are found in milk. Warm weather increases the growth rate of these bacteria. These organisms produce lactic acid, too much of which causes the casein and lime salts in the milk to separate - a state we term 'curdling' - and the milk goes sour.

What are isobars?

Isobars are found on weather maps and connect places with the same barometric pressure.

What causes thunder?

Thunder is caused by the sudden heating and expanding of the air, followed by a rapid cooling and contraction when lightning flashes. This causes the air to vibrate. The rumbling sound comes from echoes rebounding from the Earth's surface or from clouds. A long roll of thunder occurs because the sound from different parts of the electrical discharge reaches the observer at different times.

How does it rain?

If a cloud starts to cool, its vapour condenses, forming the droplets. They grow larger and larger, until they are too heavy to be held up by air currents, then they fall to the ground as rain.

How are clouds formed?

When warm air rises and reaches a particular height, it begins to cool and this causes some of the water vapour in the atmosphere to condense into droplets. A cloud is simply a large number of these droplets and is kept up in the sky by the air currents.

Who invented the lightning conductor?

The lightning conductor was invented by Benjamin Franklin. It is a rod of metal attached to the top of a tall building so the lightning does not hit the building itself.

Why did Benjamin Franklin fly a kite during a thunderstorm?

In 1752 the great American statesman and scientist attached a key to the end of a kite line and flew the kite during a thunderstorm. The key gave off sparks when lightning struck, thus proving that lightning is an electrical discharge. It was a very dangerous experiment and people have been killed trying to copy it.

Calendar Facts

What are the Ides of March?

In the Roman calendar, the Ides were the 13th or 15th day of the month. The Ides of March, however, are still remembered because Julius Caesar was killed on that day. He was warned by a fortune teller to "Beware the Ides of March" and was stabbed at a meeting of the Roman senate on 15th March 44 BC.

What are the months of the year named after?

The origins of the calendar months go back to the time of the ancient Romans. The names are Latin in origin, some in honour of famous people and some according to the order in which the months occur. This last method of naming has left us with a rather curious result: September, October, November and December are the 9th, 10th, 11th, and 12th months but their names come from Latin words meaning 7th, 8th, 9th and 10th. This happened because at one time the Roman calendar had only ten months and began with March. Around 700 BC the calendar was reformed and two months added at the beginning of the year, January and February. January is named after the god Janus, who had two faces and looked two ways at once: backwards at the old year and forwards to the new. Another god, Februus, gave us the name for February. March took its name from Mars, the god of war. April came from Latin word aperture, meaning an opening, signifying the month in which plants open and grow after winter. The origins of May and June are less certain. May was probably named after the goddess Maia, whose name meant 'nurse' or 'mother'. June may have connections with Juno, the goddess of women. July and August are named in honour of famous Romans: July for Julius Caesar and August for Augustus Caesar, the first Roman emperor.

How were the days named?

Four of the names we use for the days of the week are of Scandinavian origin, while the others come from heavenly bodies. Sunday is named in honour of the Sun; Monday was the day of the Moon; Tuesday was the day of Tiw, the Scandinavian god of war; Wednesday comes from Woden (Odin), chief of the Scandinavian gods; Thursday is named after Thor, the god of thunder; Freya (or Frigga), the goddess of friendship, gave her name to Friday; and Saturday was the day of Saturn.

Thor, the God of thunder

Why are there 24 hours in a day?

The ancient Egyptians divided daytime into ten parts marked on a sundial. At night they divided the stars into twelve groups that appeared in the night sky one after the other. Neither of these methods of calculating time was suitable at dawn or dusk, so these were added to the 22 divisions to make a total of 24. The system has also been traced to the Babylonians, who are thought to have been the first to divide daylight into 12 hours, a similar division being applied to the period of darkness.

Why does February have 29 days in a leap year?

About 2000 years ago Julius Caesar reorganised the calendar by adding an extra day every fourth year, following the advice of the Greek astronomer Sosigenes. This was necessary because the Earth takes 365 days, 5 hours, 48 minutes and 46 seconds to travel around the Sun. The Romans had found that, with a year being only 365 days, festivals did not keep in line with the seasons.

In 1582 Pope Gregory XIII made the system more acc-urate by ruling that the century years (eg: 1700, 1800, 1900, etc.) should not be treated as leap years unless they were divisible by 400. So there was not a 29th February in 1900 but there was one in the year 2000.

29 feb

What was the first boat?

It is thought a log hollowed out by fire or with a stone axe was Man's first proper boat. Early Man also lashed logs together with vines to make rafts. Initially, hands were used as oars, but it was soon discovered that wood was far more effective.

What happened to the Mary Celeste?

On 5th December 1872, the two-masted ship the Mary Celeste was found adrift in the Atlantic. Everything was as it should be - the sails were fine, there was plenty of fresh water and food on board and the cargo was still in the hold - but there was no-one on board. The ship was completely deserted. Breakfast was laid out on the table in the captain's cabin but it looked as if it had been abandoned halfway through. To this day no-one knows for certain what happened to all those on board.

What is Davy Jones' locker?

When sailors say that someone has 'gone to Davy Jones' locker', it means they have drowned. Davy Jones' locker is the ocean itself and Davy Jones is regarded as one of the spirits of the sea. It is thought the name 'Jones' came from the biblical story of Jonah, who was swallowed by a whale. It is possible the name 'Davy' came from the West Indian word 'duppy', meaning 'devil'.

Who invented the hovercraft?

The hovercraft was invented by Christopher Cokerell. To try out his theories, his first test model was made from a tin can, a coffee tin and a hairdryer.

Why is a ship's speed measured in knots?

A knot is the speed of one nautical mile per hour. In days gone by, the speed of a ship was measured by letting out a rope attached to a log. There were knots along the rope and a sailor would count these as he allowed the rope to slip through his hands. The ship's speed was the number of knots passed within a given time.

What are flotsam and jetsam?

Both words refer to wreckage or other property floating in the sea. The difference between them is that 'flotsam' are items floating on the surface accidentally, whereas 'jetsam' are items that have been deliberately thrown overboard to lighten a sinking ship.

What is a nautical mile?

A nautical or sea mile is slightly longer than a land mile. It measures 1,852 metres (approximately 2,025 yds).

What was the Spanish Armada?

A fleet of 130 ships, sent to England in 1588 by King Philip II of Spain. The main purpose was to spread the Roman Catholic religion. The king was also afraid that England was too strong, putting the land he owned in the Netherlands under threat. Lastly, it was a chance for the Spanish to get revenge on the English, who had been attacking Spanish treasure ships the world over.

What was the first steam vessel to cross the Atlantic?

The first steam-powered vessel to cross the Atlantic was the Savannah in 1819. However, it used steam power only for the start and finish of the journey, relying on sails for the rest of the voyage. Nineteen years later, the Sirius became the first ship to make the entire Atlantic crossing using steam.

Why is a ship's log book so called?

When the distance a ship has travelled is calculated from the line of knots, it is entered in a log book, named because of the log at the end of the line.

What is Semaphore?

Semaphore is a signalling system using two flags. The ways in which the flags are held represent the letters of the alphabet. The system was adopted by the British navy in about 1816, as a means for ships to communicate with one another.

What was the most famous flag signal ever flown?

Probably, the most famous flag signal was that flown by Admiral Nelson from the Victory before the Battle of Trafalgar in 1805. It read 'England expects that every man will do his duty'.

How do ships use flags to send messages?

There is an international code for the different coloured and patterned flags flown by ships. Messages can be sent from ship to ship, or ship to shore, by flying the flags in order. Some individual flags also mean particular messages as well as representing a letter.

Why are ships launched with champagne?

Launching a ship by breaking a bottle of champagne or wine across the bows is said to be the modern equivalent of an ancient sacrifice to the gods. In times gone by, the blood of an animal, or even human blood, was often used for this purpose in the hope that the gods would be so pleased with the gift, they would protect the ship at all times.

When was a coconut used to launch a ship?

In 1937 the 4,000 tonne passenger vessel El Medina was launched at Glasgow by the High Commissioner for India. To launch the ship he used a coconut, rather than champagne, as the ship would be carrying Mohammedan pilgrims, whose religion forbids the consumption of alcohol.

Who was the first man to fly solo around the world?

Wiley Hardemann Post. He took off from Floyd Bennett Field, New York, on 15th July 1933. He returned to the same airfield on 22nd July, having covered 25,099 kilometres (15,596 miles) in a flying time of 115 hours, 26 minutes.

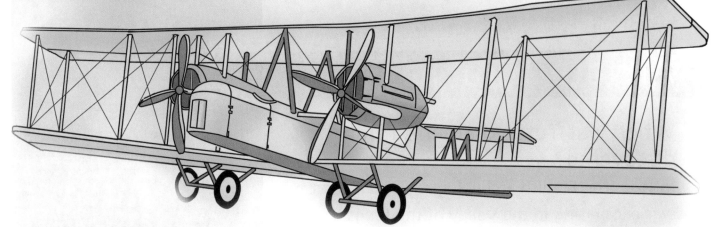

Who invented the jet plane?

The idea of jet propulsion was first proposed early in the 20th century. Frank Whittle, an officer cadet at RAF Cranwell, formulated the theory of jet-powered flight. It was not, however, until 1929 that he solved the basic problems associated with high-speed flying. He applied for a patent in 1930 and, on 12th April 1937, he saw the first test-bed run of his jet engine. Development continued over the following years but, in spite of this pioneering work, Whittle was not the first to get a jet aeroplane off the ground. The first jet-powered flight was made by a Heinkel He 178 at Marienehe, Germany, in August 1939, with an engine designed by Dr Hans von Ohain.

Who were Wilbur and Orville Wright?

They were two American brothers who designed and flew the first powered aircraft, in 1903.

Who was the first person to fly across the Atlantic?

Actually there were two people: Captain John Alcock and Lieutenant Arthur Whitten-Brown. In 1913 the newspaper publisher Lord North-cliffe offered a prize of £10,000 for the first non-stop flight across the Atlantic Ocean. As it was only four years after the first flight across the English Channel, an Atlantic flight of 3,060 kms (1,901 miles) was thought to be impossible - especially as aircraft at the time had a top range of only 1,500 kilometres (932 miles)!

At the end of the First World War, aeronautical engineers began seriously considering the Atlantic challenge. A chief test pilot, John Alcock, had given the problem a great deal of thought while a prisoner of war. By chance he met Arthur Whitten-Brown who, while in hospital during the war, had studied aerial navigation. They both took off from Newfoundland, Canada, in June 1919, in their plane powered by two Rolls Royce engines. After a hazardous journey they crashed into an Irish bog, gaining a permanent place in the history of aviation.

Atlantic Ocean

Architectural Landmarks

When was Tutankhamen's tomb discovered?

In 1922, the English archeologist Howard Carter was excavating in the Valley of the Kings at Thebes, in Egypt. On 4th November, some steps were discovered and later investigation revealed these to be the entrance to the tomb of Tutankhamen.

What is the Acropolis?

The word 'acropolis' is Greek for the upper part of a town, often a fortress on the top of a hill. Many towns had an acropolis but today the name usually refers to just one - the Acropolis in Athens - parts of which, dating from the 5th century BC, remain to this day.

What is unusual about Haydn's Tomb?

The tomb of the famous composer Franz Joseph Haydn lies at Eisenstadt, Austria. It is unusual because the composer's body is not in it. His body lies in the crypt of the church and his skull is at the museum in Vienna.

What is Cleopatra's Needle?

First of all Cleopatra's Needle, along the River Thames in London, has nothing to do with Cleopatra! The 21 metre (69 ft) high pillar is one of a pair, made 1,500 years before Cleopatra was born. One was given by the Egyptian government to Britain in 1878; the other was given to the USA and is in Central Park, New York.

What was the original purpose of London's Marble Arch?

Marble Arch was first built as the main entrance to Buckingham Palace. However, it was not wide enough for a stagecoach to get through, so it was moved to its present site near Hyde Park.

What is the largest inhabited castle in the world?

Windsor Castle in England. Much of it was built in the 11th century by William the Conqueror and it is now the official home of the British monarch.

Where is the oldest bridge?

It is thought the clapper bridges (made of large stones placed on boulders) on Exmoor and Dartmoor, are of prehistoric origin - but none can be dated with any certainty. The oldest bridge that can be dated is a stone arch bridge in Izmir, Turkey, which was built almost 3,000 years ago.

How did the White House get its name?

Washington, USA, was captured by British forces during the Anglo-American War of 1812 and many buildings were burned. One such building was the President's mansion. To conceal the damage, the building was given a quick coat of whitewash. The Presidential residence has been known as the White House ever since.

What was the original purpose of the London Monument?

This tall column was designed by Christopher Wren. It commemorates the Great Fire of London of 1666, although it was originally intended to be a telescope. The column was built to house a large lens presented to the Royal Academy by the Dutch scientist Christiaan Huygens but the tube was too short. Wren then built a staircase inside and it became the London Monument!

How high is the Monument?

It is thought that the height of the Monument, 62 metres (203 ft), is exactly the same as the distance from its base to the site where the Great Fire began.

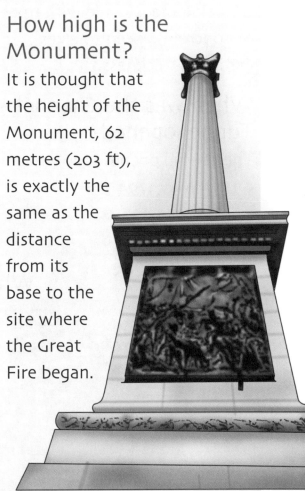

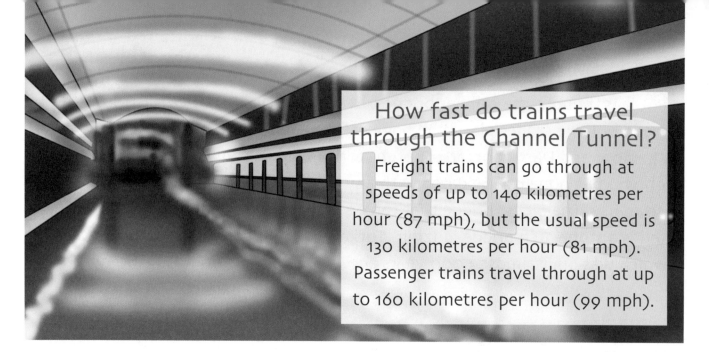

How fast do trains travel through the Channel Tunnel?

Freight trains can go through at speeds of up to 140 kilometres per hour (87 mph), but the usual speed is 130 kilometres per hour (81 mph). Passenger trains travel through at up to 160 kilometres per hour (99 mph).

Could the tunnel collapse?

The tunnel is lined with reinforced concrete that can withstand the force of a bomb or an earthquake, so there is no chance of it collapsing. The tunnel lining is made with rings of concrete 45 centimetres (18 in) in thickness.

When was the Channel Tunnel opened?

The official opening took place on 6th May 1994.

How deep is the Channel Tunnel?

There are actually three tunnels: two single-track rail tunnels and one two-track service tunnel. The three tunnels run for 50 kilometres (31 miles), and run between 23 metres (75 ft) to 46 metres (151 ft) below the sea.

Who had a palace of ice?

In 1739, Empress Anna of Russia had a novel palace built - it was made entirely of ice.

Where is the Bridge of Sighs?

The Bridge of Sighs is a famous covered bridge in Venice. It crosses the Rio di Palazzo and joins the Doges' Palace with the old state prison. Its name comes from the sadness of the prisoners as they walked to their cells.

Who built the Sphinx?

Egypt has many statues of sphinxes. These represent imaginary animals with a lion's body and the head of a man. They were built as shrines to Egyptian gods. The most famous sphinx lies at Giza and was built on the orders of King Khafra in about 2,600 BC.

Construction Material

How are bricks made?

There are three basic ways in which bricks can be made. In the first, water is mixed with clay into a paste which is forced into wooden moulds. The mixture is then tipped out and placed in giant ovens called kilns. The second method involves forming a very stiff clay mixture which is forced through a rectangular hole before being cut into brick-sized pieces with a wire. The third method is similar to the first, but less water is used and the bricks are pressed into shape. The first process is known as the 'stock method' because the wooden moulds are called stocks; the second is known as the 'wire-cut' process; and the third is called the 'semi-dry' process.

Once the bricks are moulded into shape, they are placed in kilns to be fired, a process that takes several days, during which the bricks are subjected to a very high temperature. Most modern brick manufacturers use a continuous chamber kiln through which the bricks travel, so that by the time they come out from the other end of the kiln, they have been completely fired and are ready for use.

Why do bricks overlap?

If you look at a brick building, you will see that the bricks are not laid directly on top of one another. If they were, the building would soon fall down! Bricks are overlapped so that each brick supports its neighbours and there are no continuous vertical joins.

How is concrete delivered ready-mixed?

The various ingredients of cement are loaded into a large mixer on the back of a lorry. As a lorry is driven to a building site, the mixer rotates and mixes the ingredients - sand, cement, gravel and water. By the time the lorry arrives at the site, the concrete is ready for use.

Law & Administration

Which is the world's oldest parliament?

The Althing is the parliament of Iceland. It has been in existence since the 10th century making it the oldest parliament in history.

What is Hansard?

Hansard is the name given to the official reports of events in the House of Commons. It gets its name from Luke Hansard, who started a House of Commons Journal in 1774.

Is fingerprinting a modern technique?

No. The ancient Chinese used fingerprinting as a means of identification. The ancient Babylonians made fingerprints in clay.

Who first suggested using fingerprints to catch criminals?

Henry Faulds, a Scottish physician, in a letter he had published in Nature magazine in October 1880.

TAX NOT PAID

What was the Window Tax?

It was a tax, first levied in 1696, on the number of windows in a house. The tax remained in force until 1851, although the number of windows liable to tax varied. People who did not want to pay simply bricked up some of their windows, which can still be seen on some old houses today.

What was the Nose Tax?

No, it was not a tax on people's noses! It was a tax of one ounce of gold to be paid by every householder in Ireland during the 9th century. The tax was successfully levied by the Danes for 13 years until the officials were massacred. The tax obtained its curious name because anyone who refused or was unable to pay the tax had his nose slit in punishment.

What was the gunpowder plot?

It was a plan to blow up British Parliament on the first day of a new session, when King James I and all his ministers would be present. The plot was designed to be the start of an armed uprising against the persecution of Catholics in England. The plot failed because one of the conspirators, Francis Tresham, warned a friend not to attend Parliament on that day and all the plotters were arrested.

What is a democracy?

Democracy is a form of government in which the people of a country decide future events. This is usually done by the population electing persons to represent their views in the government. The word comes from two Greek words, 'demos' (people) and 'kratos' (power). The former American president Abraham Lincoln described it as "government of the people, by the people and for the people".

Who were the Bow Street Runners?

Established in 1749, by the novelist Henry Fielding, the Bow Street Runners were a group of law officers attached to Bow Street court in London. As they wore scarlet waistcoats, they were nicknamed Robin Redbreasts. Police forces as we know them today did not yet exist. The Bow Street Runners thus created a new respect for law and order and had considerable success in catching wrong-doers.

What was 'hue and cry'?

In Anglo-Saxon times official police forces, like we have today, had yet to be formed. It was therefore the duty of each person to raise a 'hue and cry' if he or she saw a crime being committed. When that happened everyone had to stop what they were doing and chase the criminal. This system continued in Britain with very little change until well into the 17th century.

What is woolsack?

The woolsack is the seat of the Lord Chancellor, used when he is presiding over the sittings of the House of Lords in London. At an early date, a sack of wool was used as a seat. During the reign of Henry VIII, the Chancellor and other high officials sat upon such sacks. Today, the woolsack is a large square cushion of wool, covered with red cloth. The use of the woolsack for this purpose reflects the vital part which the wool trade once played in the British economy.

Which British Prime Minister was assassinated?

Spencer Perceval, elected in 1809. Three years later, he was walking through the House of Commons when he was shot dead by John Bellingham, who had a grudge against the government.

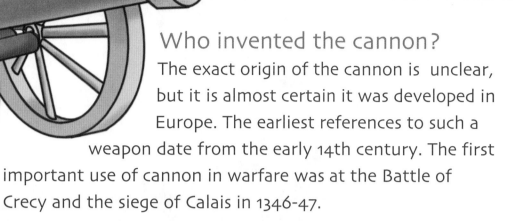

Who invented the cannon?

The exact origin of the cannon is unclear, but it is almost certain it was developed in Europe. The earliest references to such a weapon date from the early 14th century. The first important use of cannon in warfare was at the Battle of Crecy and the siege of Calais in 1346-47.

How did a bucket start a war?

In the year 1325, a group of men from the state of Modena, Italy, stole a wooden bucket from the state of Bologna. This resulted in a fight between the two groups that developed into a 12 year war.

What were early cannons made of?

The barrels of early cannons were made of wood and leather strengthened by iron bands. They fired stone cannon balls.

Why do soldiers salute?

In the Middle Ages, it was the custom for knights in armour to raise their visors when meeting someone, as a sign of respect and friendship. Although modern soldiers do not have visors like the knights of old, the salute is still performed as a sign of respect.

Which is the oldest army?

The oldest army in the world is that of the Swiss Guard in the Vatican City, Rome, Italy. Its origins date back to at least the 15th century

What was the Maginot Line?

Named after Andre Maginot (French Minister of War), this line of fortifications was built between 1929 and 1934 along the French border with Luxembourg and Switzerland. When the Germans invaded France in 1940, they entered through Belgium, a region not protected by the Maginot Line.

What is the shortest war on record?

At 9.02 am on 27th August 1896, Britain declared war on Zanzibar. After just 38 minutes of bombardment the Sultan of Zanzibar surrendered.

What is the longest war on record?

The Hundred Years' War, which began between France and England in 1337. It is known as 'The Hundred Years' War' but it actually lasted 116 years!

Where is the Mason-Dixon line?

The Mason-Dixon Line is a boundary that separated the northern and southern states before the American Civil War. It was established by the Penn family, of Pennsylvania and the Calvert family, who owned Maryland. The two families argued continually about where the boundary should be. Eventually, they agreed to employ two Englishmen, Charles Mason and Jeremiah Dixon, to survey the boundary. The work was finished in 1767, and still exists as the boundary between the states of Maryland, Pennsylvania and part of West Virginia.

How did a cockerel help win a battle?

During the battle of St Vincent in 1797, the British ship HMS Marlborough was so badly damaged, the officers considered surrendering. The captain and the lieutenant had been wounded and the ship dismasted. Then a shot from the Spanish fleet hit the kitchen coop on board. A cockerel found sudden freedom, fluttered over what was left of the damaged mainmast and gave a hearty crow. The ship's company responded with three loud cheers, and with their morale heightened went back into action with renewed vigour.

What was the mutiny on the Bounty?

In 1787, Captain William Bligh commanded HMS Bounty to the South Pacific. He was so strict the crew mutinied, setting him adrift with 18 men. The mutineers settled in Tahiti and on Pitcairn Island, where some of their descendants live to this day.

Who led the mutiny on the Bounty?

Fletcher Christian, the mate on HMS Bounty, led the mutiny against the harsh regime of Captain Bligh. After the mutiny, Christian settled on Pitcairn Island in the Pacific.

How was a city saved by a bowl of soup?

During the siege of Geneva, Switzerland, in the 16th century, a housewife heard the enemy climbing the city walls. She prevented them from entering the city by pouring a cauldron of boiling soup over them.

What happened to Captain Bligh?

After being cast adrift by the crew, Bligh and his supporters sailed 5,822 kilometres (3,618 miles) to Timor Island, near Java. They managed this without charts and very little food. On his return to England, Bligh reported the mutiny. In 1805 he was appointed Governor of New South Wales, Australia, where once again, his strict discipline caused a mutiny in 1808. On returning to England, he was made an admiral.

How did a football match start a war?

The supporters of El Salvador and Honduras began fighting each other during a football match in 1969. The brawl was quite serious, and developed rapidly into full scale war between the two countries.

What was 'The War of Jenkins' Ear'?

On 9th April 1731, Spanish coastguards boarded the ship Rebecca off the coast of Havana, Cuba. They cut off the ear of the captain, Robert Jenkins, and tied him to the mast before setting the ship adrift. In 1738, he told his story to the British House of Commons and it provided an excuse for a naval war with Spain which lasted from 1739 to 1742. This became known as 'The War of Jenkins' Ear'.

What was the Boston tea party?

When the British imposed taxes on tea imported by America in the 18th century, the people of Boston decided to refuse delivery of the goods. But when the tea ships would not leave, the Bostonians took drastic action. After dusk on 16th December 1773, a band of men disguised as Native Americans slipped aboard the ships in Boston Harbor, broke open the tea chests and threw all the tea into the water.

How did the great fire of London start?

On 2nd September 1666, a small fire was discovered in a wooden house in Pudding Lane. The house belonged to the King's baker, John Farynore. It raged on for four days and destroyed a vast area of London.

How many people died in the great fire of London?

Thankfully, although a vast area of the city was destroyed, only six people were killed in the fire.

When did a horse choose a king?

In AD 522 Persia was left without a king after the death of Cambyses. Various contenders for the crown decided to meet on horseback at sunrise - the man whose horse neighed first would become king. One such contender was Darius Hystaspes, whose groom took his horse to the meeting spot and allowed it to become fond of a mare that was grazing there. The next day, Darius' horse immediately neighed for the mare - and Darius was chosen as king.

When was the RNLI founded?

The RNLI was formed in 1824 when a meeting in London resolved " . . . that an institution be now formed for the Preservation of Life in cases of Shipwreck on the Coasts of the United Kingdom, to be supported by donations and annual subscription; and to be called the National Institution for the Preservation of Life from Shipwreck." The name was changed to the Royal National Lifeboat Institution 30 years later.

Which British institution began in a coffee house?

In 1698 the London dealers in company stocks and shares arranged to meet in Jonathan's Coffee House. It was the start of what was to become the London Stock Exchange. As a result of this unusual first meeting place, the messengers in the Stock Exchange are still called 'waiters'.

What was the Magna Carta?

'Magna Carta' is Latin for 'Great Charte'. It was a document approved by King John at Runnymede in 1215. Because of the cruel manner in which he treated the English people and his demand for money to help fight his wars, King John was not popular. The Barons were particularly against the king because he demanded large payments from them. Eventually they revolted and drew up an agreement which the king accepted. This document, the Articles of the Barons, was converted into a Royal Charter which was sent to the sheriff of every county in the land. Commonly known as the Magna Carta, it had a great influence on history and marked the first steps to constitutional government - a government according to law.

When did Prince Charles become the Prince of Wales?

In 1958, when he was almost ten. Charles was invested at Caernafon Castle on 1st July 1969. He is the 21st heir apparent to bear the title.

Amazing People

Why do people sometimes shout 'Geronimo!' before making a great jump?

Geronimo was an American Indian chief. When escaping from the US Cavalry, he made a daring leap from a high cliff into a river. As he fell, he yelled his name. This incident was then depicted in a 1940 film and during the Second World War, American paratroopers began shouting 'Geronimo!' when they jumped.

Which US President could write two languages at the same time?

Quite a lot of people are ambidextrous meaning they can write with both their right and left hands. Some people have developed this ability so they can write with both hands at the same time. But James Abraham Garfield, President of the USA from 1880-81, took his talent one step further - he could write in Latin with one hand and in Greek with the other!

When did Queen Cleopatra die?

Cleopatra killed herself in 30 BC after learning that her lover, Marcus Antonius (Mark Anthony), ruler of the eastern Roman Empire, had committed suicide. According to tradition, Cleopatra poisoned herself by making an asp bite her.

For what was Rodin famous?

Auguste Rodin was born in Paris in 1840. He was a sculptor famous for such works as The Thinker and The Kiss.

Who was Capability Brown?

Lancelot Brown was a famous landscape gardener of the 18th century. He was nicknamed 'Capability' because he would often say that a place had 'capabilities of improvement'.

Who were the first known people to sail around the world?

The surviving crew of the Victoria. The vessel left Spain in 1519 and returned in 1522. Sadly, the navigator, Ferdinand Magellan, did not complete the journey. He was killed by natives in the Philippines in 1521.

Who was Edith Cavell?

Edith Louisa Cavell was born in Norfolk in 1865. She grew up to become a nurse and moved to Brussels in 1907. During the First World War, she and her colleague, Philippe Baucq, helped English and French soldiers escape to Holland. Cavell was arrested in 1915, and she and Baucq were condemned to death.

Who was Tom Thumb?

His real name was Charles Sherwood Stratton. He was born on 4th January 1838 and died on 15th July 1883. Stratton became famous as General Tom Thumb because he was only 1 metre (about 3 ft) tall.

Who was Guy Fawkes?

He was born in 1570. His name is remembered to this day because he was part of the Gunpowder Plot of 1605, a scheme to blow up the Houses of Parliament in London.

Who were the Luddites?

In the early 19th century, many factory workers rioted in protest to new machinery that was replacing them in the factories. Their leader was General Ludd and the rioters became known as Luddites. However, it turned out there was no such person as General Ludd - it was just a name the rioters had made up!

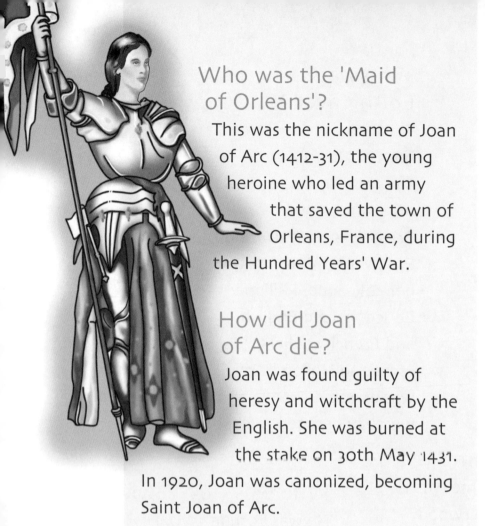

Who was the 'Maid of Orleans'?

This was the nickname of Joan of Arc (1412-31), the young heroine who led an army that saved the town of Orleans, France, during the Hundred Years' War.

How did Joan of Arc die?

Joan was found guilty of heresy and witchcraft by the English. She was burned at the stake on 30th May 1431. In 1920, Joan was canonized, becoming Saint Joan of Arc.

Who was Kublai Khan?

Kublai Khan (1215-1294), grandson of Genghis Khan, was one of the great rulers in world history. When his brother died in 1259, he became the great emperor of the Mongol Empire. By 1279, he had conquered the entire country. He tried to expand his empire to include Java and Japan but his invasions of these countries were unsuccessful.

Who was Tutankhamen?

Tutankhamen was an Egyptian pharaoh who lived from 1361 to 1352 BC. He is often called 'the boy pharaoh' because he was only nine when he became king.

When did Napoleon become famous?

Napoleon is now best known for his extraordinary military campaigns. Yet he was a national figure in France long before what became known as the Napoleonic Wars. He was a capable artillery commander when, in 1795, he came to the attention of the government as a man to be relied on. Appointed second-in-command of the army of the interior, he was largely responsible for crushing a royalist rising.

Who were the Pankhursts?

Emmeline Pankhurst and her daughters, Christabel and Sylvia, were the leaders of the English suffragette movement (the fight for voting rights for women). Their campaigns were often militant and all three women were frequently arrested. The campaign was a success and women were eventually granted the right to vote.

Who was Confucius?

K'ung Fu-Tzu was a Chinese teacher who lived from about 551 to 479 BC. The Latin version of his name is Confucius, the name used by Jesuit missionaries in China. His teachings formed the basis of Confucianism, a guide to life followed by many people of China.

Who was Lawrence of Arabia?

T E Lawrence was a British archaeologist and soldier who worked on excavations in Egypt from 1911-14. He then became an intelligence officer in Cairo and later, joined the Arab revolt against the Turks. He lived with and dressed like the Arabs, and became known as Lawrence of Arabia.

Who was Mata Hari?

Mata Hari, whose real name was Margaretha Geertruida Zelle, was born in 1876. From 1905, she was a professional dancer and also acted as a spy for both the French and the Germans during the First World War.

Who was Saint Valentine?

The most likely saint after whom 'valentines' are named was a Roman priest. Under the persecution of Claudius the Goth, St. Valentine was beheaded in about 269 AD. There are three other St. Valentines, any one of whom could be the person after whom valentine cards were named. Unfortunately, none of the four had much connection with love.

When did St Valentine's day customs originate?

St Valentine's Day customs originally developed from the Roman festival of Lupercalia, which took place each February.

Who was Marco Polo?

Marco Polo (1254-1324) was an Italian merchant from Venice. In 1271, he joined his father and uncle on an overland journey to the Far East. Polo ended up staying in China for 17 years, employed by the emperor, Kublai Khan, for official missions. He eventually returned to Italy by sea (1292-1295).

Who was 'The Iron Duke'?

The Iron Duke was a nickname of the Duke of Wellington. It actually came from an iron vessel called Duke of Wellington, which was launched in Victorian times. As such metal vessels were unusual then, it was called 'The Iron Duke'.

Who was the 'Lady with the Lamp'?

This nickname was given to a nurse who tended the injured during the Crimean War, which ended in 1856. She was Florence Nightingale, and was nicknamed 'The Lady with the Lamp' because she carried a lamp as she checked on her patients during the night.

Were there ever any female pirates?

There were quite a few well-known women pirates in the 17th century. The two most famous were Anne Bonny and Mary Read.

Who was John Bull?

John Bull was a symbol of the British people and was even a nickname for Britain itself. The name first appeared in comics after Dr John Arbuthnott published a book called The History of John Bull (1712).

Who was El Cid?

Rodrigo Diaz de Vivar was born in about 1043 in Castile, Spain. He became a national hero when he fought against the Moors. He was known to Spaniards as 'el Campeador' (the champion) but the Moors called him 'el Cid' (the Lord).

Who was Bonnie Prince Charlie?

When James II fled England in 1688, leaving the throne to the Protestant William of Orange, he took with him his baby son, who was then only six months old. This baby, also called James, grew up in exile, calling himself James III. It was his son, christened Charles Edward, who was the Bonnie Prince Charlie of history. He landed in Scotland in 1745 and led a rising against the reigning king, George II. When the rising was finally crushed, at Culloden in 1746, the discouraged Prince sailed away into exile.

Who was Sitting Bull?

Sitting Bull, who also appeared in Buffalo Bill's Wild West Show, was an American Indian chief. He led the Sioux at the Battle of the Little Bighorn in 1876, where they defeated the 7th Cavalry commanded by General Custer.

Who was Annie Oakley?

Annie Oakley, who starred in Buffalo Bill's Wild West Show, was a crack shot with guns. She even beat the American marksman Frank E Butler, who later became her husband.

Who were the Tolpuddle Martyrs?

A group of six labourers from Dorset who were unhappy with their poor working conditions formed a union to improve them. Although this was not illegal, the government decided the union could lead to unrest and in 1834 they were exiled to Australia for seven years. Public opinion against the sentences proved so great that the men were pardoned in 1836.

Who was Buffalo Bill?

Buffalo Bill's Wild West Show was formed in 1883. It was a spectacular circus featuring cowboys and Indians who toured all over the USA and Europe. Among the stars were Annie Oakley, Sitting Bull and Buffalo Bill. Buffalo Bill claimed he had earned his nickname because he had shot over 4,000 bisons to help feed men who were building a railroad.

Interesting Inventions

What is a patent?

A patent is a licence issued by a government office to a person or company giving the right to make or sell an invention. If an inventor wants to stop other people copying his invention, he has to apply to the Patent Office with a full description of the invention. The application is then checked against the records to make sure that the idea is original, and has not been copied from another inventor.

How does a Yale Lock work?

A Yale lock consists of a narrow cylinder revolving inside a larger, fixed cylinder. When the key is inserted into the keyhole the notches on the key push up a series of pins until they are all at the same level. This allows the key to turn, moving the inner cylinder and pulling back the bolt of the lock. The pins in each lock are different, so each has its own individual key.

Who invented the first lock?

The first locks were invented over 4,000 years ago by the Chinese, but the ancient Egyptians also had quite intricate locks. They were often very large and usually consisted of a large bolt that was moved into a staple by a big key.

Who invented the Yale Lock?

Linus Yale Jr. invented the cylinder lock now known as the Yale, in the 1860s. The big advantage of the Yale lock compared with other locks of the day was its superb engineering and the fact that it was smaller than any other key. As a result, Yale locks became popular the world over.

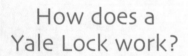

Who invented the kite?

The first kite is said to have been invented by a Chinese farmer whose hat blew off in the wind. He tied a string to it and the next time it blew off he had a kite!

When was knitting invented?

Knitting appears to have originated in Arabia over 3,000 years ago. Some items knitted by nomadic tribesmen of that period exist to this day.

Who invented the safety pin?

People in the Middle Ages secured their clothing with pins of various types but it was not until 1849 that the modern safety pin was developed. It was invented by Walter Hunt of New York in order to repay someone 15 dollars. It took him just three hours to come up with the idea.

Who invented the bowler hat?

In 1849, William Coke designed a hat that was so strong he could stamp on it without causing damage. It was made for him by hat-makers Thomas and William Bowler. The hat became very popular but instead of being called a 'coke' after its inventor, it attracted the name of 'bowler' from the people who made it.

Who invented the paperclip?

It was Johann Vaaler of Norway, who patented his invention in 1900.

Who invented cat's-eyes?

Percy Shaw was driving late one night in 1934, when he thought of an idea that would revolutionise road travel. But his suggestion to put reflective studs on the roads did not appeal to the authorities. During the 'blackout' of the Second World War, car headlights had to be masked. This made it more difficult for drivers to see the road and 'cat's-eyes' were introduced on a large scale. Although the cat's-eyes were visible to the vehicle driver, they did not cast any light upward, so they could not be seen by enemy aircraft. This simple device is now used on roads all over the world.

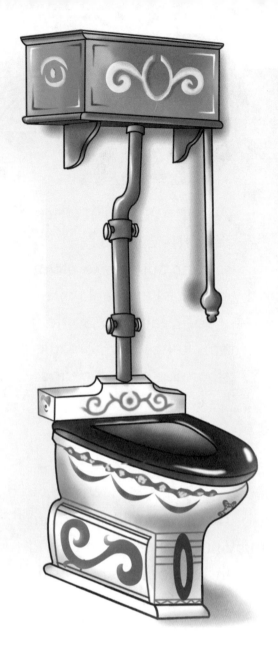

Who invented the flush toilet?

The ancient Egyptians, Greeks and Roman all had toilets with flushing systems, but by the Middle Ages these had been forgotten. The first 'modern' flush toilet was designed by Sir John Harrington in 1589. It is thought only two were made, one for his own home and one for his godmother, Queen Elizabeth I.

Who invented the mackintosh?

In 1823 a Scottish chemist, Charles Mackintosh, discovered a way to dissolve rubber with a chemical called naptha. He sandwiched this rubber between two pieces of cloth to make a waterproof material. This material was too stiff to sew, but James Syme, a young medical student, found a new way to dissolve the rubber which made it softer and therefore easier to sew together to make raincoats.

Who invented Braille?

Louis Braille lost his sight when he was just a young boy. It was while working with leather, using his father's awl, that he came up with the idea of a raised writing system. He had used the awl to punch holes in leather and knew that if the awl did not go all the way through, it raised a prominent bump on the underside of the material. Blind people would be able to feel this bump and Braille turned his attention to developing a system of six raised dots that could be formed to represent letters. Braille's system was devised in 1824.

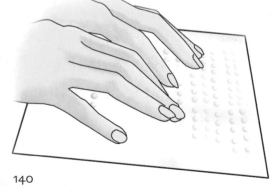

Who invented Christmas cards?

In 1843, Sir Henry Cole decided to get in touch with all his friends at Christmas, but didn't have time to write to all of them. He asked artist John Horsley to design a card instead. After sending the cards to his friends, Cole found he had some left so he sold them in a London shop. Although people had sent cards before, it was not a common practice. Cole's cards changed all that and now billions are sent out each year all around the world.

When was the mirror invented?

There are several examples in existence of mirrors used by the ancient Greeks and Romans. The oldest dates from around 400 BC and consists of a highly polished, sheet of bronze. It was not until the 16th century, when the Venetians discovered how to make glass that gave the truest reflection, that glass mirrors came into fashion.

Who invented matches?

The first match was invented by accident. John Walker, a chemist, was mixing some chemicals with a stick and some of the mixture stuck to the wood. He tried to scrape it off on the stone floor and it burst into flames. The chemist realized the importance of his discovery and was soon making matches to sell in his shop. The first person to buy some was a solicitor, called Mr Hixon, who bought a box of Walker's matches on 7th April 1827.

Who invented the Christmas cracker?

Tom Smith, a London sweet maker, was looking for a novelty for his sweets in 1846. A piece of wood cracked in his fire and this inspired him to invent the 'snap' that is used in crackers. The first crackers contained sweets.

141

Who made the first hover mower?

The Flymo Company produced the first hover mower, based on the principle of the hovercraft, in 1963.

Who invented the pillar box?

The idea of the British pillar box was conceived by Anthony Trollope. Although now best known as a writer, Trollope was once a postal official. In 1851, he was sent to the Channel Islands to inspect postal services. He found that people had to walk long distances to post letters, and suggested 'safe receptacles' be set up on the roadsides. Trollope had seen public mail boxes in France (the French adopted the idea from the Belgians, who first used mail boxes in 1849).

When was the first electric lawn mower developed?

The first patent for an electrically powered lawn mower was issued to Ransomes in 1926.

Who invented the lawn mower?

In 1805, Thomas Plucknett invented a two-wheeled machine with a circular blade, to cut grass and corn. The first mass-produced mowers were made in 1832, using a design invented by Edwin Budding two years earlier.

When was the motorized mower first produced?

The Ransomes company produced the first successful motorised lawn mower, in 1902 (although, experimental mowers had been designed in Germany and the USA several years earlier).

Who invented Worcestershire sauce?

Worcestershire sauce was created almost by accident. In 1835, Lord Sandys returned to Britain after a period of military service in India. He brought with him a recipe for a spicy Indian sauce and he asked chemists John W Lea and William Perrins to make some for him. They did so, but it tasted horrible, so they put the jars away. They forgot all about the sauce until they came across it in their cellar some time later. The pair tried it again and this time it was very tasty, having had time to mature. Lea and Perrins obtained permission to market the mixture and called it Worcestershire sauce, because they lived in Worcester.

When was glue invented?

Glue dates back to ancient Egypt. The Egyptians would boil animal bones, horns and hides - a process that is still used for making some glues today.

Who invented the dishwasher?

For ten years, Mrs W A Cockran tried to persuade her husband to give her some money to develop a dishwashing machine she had invented, but he always refused. After his death, friends lent her some money and the machine was built in 1889. The dishwasher could reportedly wash, rinse and dry dishes of various shapes and sizes in just two minutes. The water was sprayed onto the dishes by a pump which was activated by turning a handle.

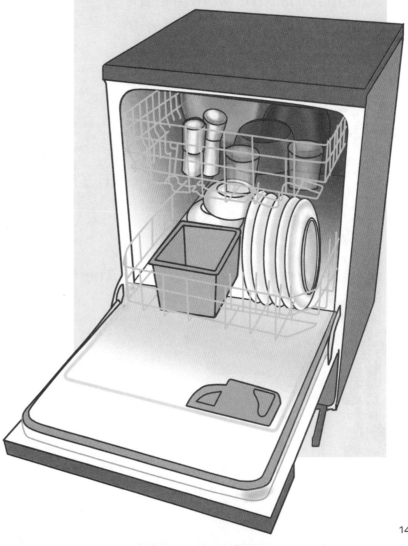

The Wonders of Technology

What is a silicon chip?

In 1953, Hardwick Johnson, of the Radio Corporation of America (RCA), built an electronic circuit on a tiny piece of germanium. By adding insulating layers on top of the germanium, it was possible to have transistors, capacitors and resistors all on the same chip - known as a silicon chip.

How was electricity discovered?

The ancient Greeks discovered that amber rubbed with a dry cloth attracted small particles of the material. The word 'electricity' comes from the Greek Word 'elecktron', meaning amber.

What was the first regular television service?

The world's first regular TV service was started by the BBC on 2nd November 1936. Transmissions ceased in 1939, two days before the outbreak of the Second World War. They re-started on 7th June 1946, the eve of the Victory parades.

Who invented television?

The Scottish electrical engineer John Logie Baird.

When did the first public television broadcast take place?

The first public television broadcast was made by the BBC on 30th September 1929.

Who made the first telephone call in Britain?

Alexander Graham Bell demonstrated the telephone in Britain on the Isle of Wight. The person to make the first call was Queen Victoria on 14th January 1878, to Sir Thomas Biddulph.

Who invented radar?

The basic principle of radar (the reflection of short radio waves) was discovered in the 1920s. But it wasn't until British scientist Robert Watson-Watt began experimenting with radio waves that this method (of detecting an object's position and speed), became a possibility. The world's first radar station opened in Britain in 1935. The word 'radar' is short for 'Radio Detecting and Ranging'.

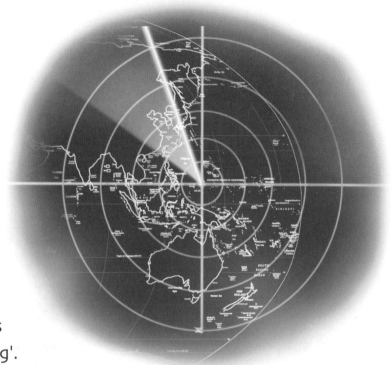

Which British town was the first to have electric street lighting?

The first proper tests of electric street lights were held in Westgate-on-Sea and London in 1878. By 1881 electric lights had been installed throughout the country.

Who was the first person to appear on television?

The first person to have his image transmitted by television was William Taynton, a 15-year-old London office boy, on 2nd October 1925. John Logie Baird had just succeeded in transmitting a picture of a ventriloquist's dummy from one room to another and wanted a live subject. Taynton happened to be the first person he saw as he rushed out to the street to find someone. But the boy was so frightened by all the lights and strange machinery that Baird had to give him some pocket money before he would submit to the experiment.

Who invented the radio?

As a child, Guglielmo Marconi of Italy was fascinated by electricity. At the age of 20, he achieved his first radio transmission - sending the three dots of Morse code letter S from one end of his attic to the other. Shortly after, he and his brother, Alfonso, were sending signals over longer distances. The Italian government were not interested in his work so Marconi went to England, where the British Post Office gave him support. On 12th December 1901, Marconi succeeded in beaming Morse code signals across the Atlantic.

What was the first entertainment broadcast?

On 12th June 1920, the Marconi Company broadcasted a recital by the opera singer Dame Nellie Melba. All further broadcasts for entertainment purposes were immediately banned, as officials thought them too trivial for such an important means of communication. In 1921, the ban was relaxed and half an hour of speech and music broadcasting was permitted each week.

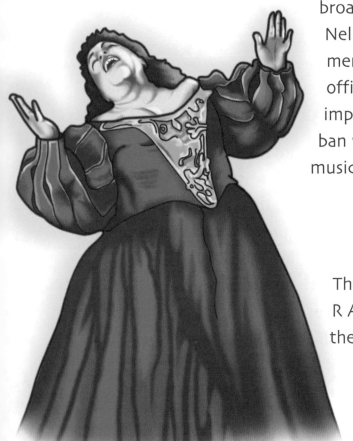

Who was the first to transmit speech by radio?

The first person to transmit speech by radio was R A Fessenden of the University of Pittsburgh in the USA. On Christmas Eve 1906, he transmitted speech and music over several hundred kilometres - the first true radio broadcast.

Where were traffic lights first used?

In the late 19th century, British politicians had trouble turning their carriages safely into the Palace of Westminster. In response, the Metropolitan Commissioner of Police, Richard Mayne, organised the introduction of a traffic control system of red and green gas-powered lights. They came into operation on 10th December, 1868. The lights were controlled by a lever at the base but its operation was unreliable. Just a few weeks after the control's installation, a police officer was injured when the apparatus exploded. The lights were unpopular and remained in service for only a few years.

What was the first computer?

Over the centuries, many machines and devices have been invented to help Man with complicated calculations. The first computer in the modern sense was the 'Analytical Engine' invented by Charles Baggage in 1834. Unfortunately, it was too difficult for Victorian engineers to make and was not built until the 1990s, by which time computers were commonplace.

Who had the first electric traffic lights?

The first electrically operated traffic lights were installed at a busy crossroad in Ohio, USA, on 5th August 1914. Drivers were warned the lights were about to change by means of a loud buzzer. The first electrically operated lights in Britain came into service in London in 1926.

What is binary?

The system of counting we use every day is based on the number ten. Binary works on the number two. There are just two digits, 1 and 0. This makes the system ideal for computers because the two digits can be represented by an electrical signal being switched off for one digit and on for the other.

0 : 0	6 : 110	12 : 1100
1 : 1	7 : 111	13 : 1101
2 : 10	8 : 1000	14 : 1110
3 : 11	9 : 1001	15 : 1111
4 : 100	10 : 1010	16 : 10000
5 : 101	11 : 1011	

The First ...

When was food first cooked?
Man first discovered cooking during the Stone Age, after learning to make fire. A caveman probably dropped a piece of meat onto a fire by accident and then found that it smelled (and tasted) rather good.

Who was the first person to be buried in St Paul's Cathedral?
St Paul's Cathedral in London was finished in 1710. Its designer, Sir Christopher Wren, died in 1723 at the age of 90. He was the first person to be buried there.

Who was the first ever English Pope?
So far only one Englishman has been Pope. He was Nicholas Breakspear, who was elected with the name Pope Adrian IV, in December 1154.

Who was the first Prince of Wales?
In 1301, King Edward I of England invested his eldest son, Edward, as the Prince of Wales. King Edward's main purpose in creating this title was probably to placate the Welsh people after his wars of conquest. Since then, the title has been conferred upon the male heir apparent of the sovereign.

When was the top hat first worn?
James Hetherington wore the first top hat in London on 5th January 1797. He was promptly arrested because his new headgear caused quite a disturbance: a huge crowd gathered round him, in which many people started to panic and even faint!

Where is the world's first iron bridge?

The world's first iron bridge spans a gorge through which the River Severn flows near Coalbrookdale in Shropshire. Built in 1779 by Abraham Darby, it remains a unique monument to the industrial revolution. It was such a remarkable structure that a small township about half a mile from Coalbrookdale was named Ironbridge. Much of the area is now a vast open-air museum.

Which was the first stagecoach to cross America?

John Butterfield's Overland Mail Company which carried mail across the USA during the 1850-60s.

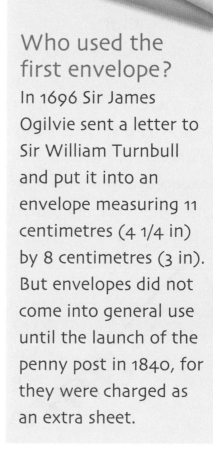

Why are flags sometimes flown at half mast?

Flags are flown at half mast as a sign of mourning and respect for someone who has recently died.

When was a flag first flown at half mast?

In 1626 James Hall, leader of an expedition to find the North-west Passage, was killed by a group of Inuit. The flag on board his ship, the Hartsease, was lowered to half mast as a mark of respect.

Who used the first envelope?

In 1696 Sir James Ogilvie sent a letter to Sir William Turnbull and put it into an envelope measuring 11 centimetres (4 1/4 in) by 8 centimetres (3 in). But envelopes did not come into general use until the launch of the penny post in 1840, for they were charged as an extra sheet.

Who was the first to run a mile in under four minutes?

In 1954 an English doctor, Roger Bannister, ran a mile in just 3 minutes 59.4 seconds. He was the first known man to break the four minute barrier.

When were houses first given numbers?

The first time houses were numbered was in 1463, on the Pont Notre-Dame in Paris.

Who was the first person to write a detective story?

'The Murders in the Rue Morgue' (published by Graham's Magazine, Philadelphia in 1841) is considered the world's first detective story. It was written by Edgar Allan Poe.

Who was the first magician?

The first person to entertain with 'magic' is unknown. The first of whom there is any definite record is Dedi, who performed before King Cheops of Egypt over 5,000 years ago. His amazing feats are detailed in an ancient papyrus which is kept in a Berlin museum.

Who made the first toothbrush?

William Addis made the first toothbrush in 1780. It did not prove very popular and the idea didn't really catch on until the late 19th century.

Who was the first person to wear roller skates?

In 1760 Joseph Merlin entered a masquerade party in London, on roller skates. Playing a violin, he glided across the room. Unfortunately, he could not stop or change direction and smashed into a large mirror. The mirror was broken, his violin was smashed and he was badly hurt!

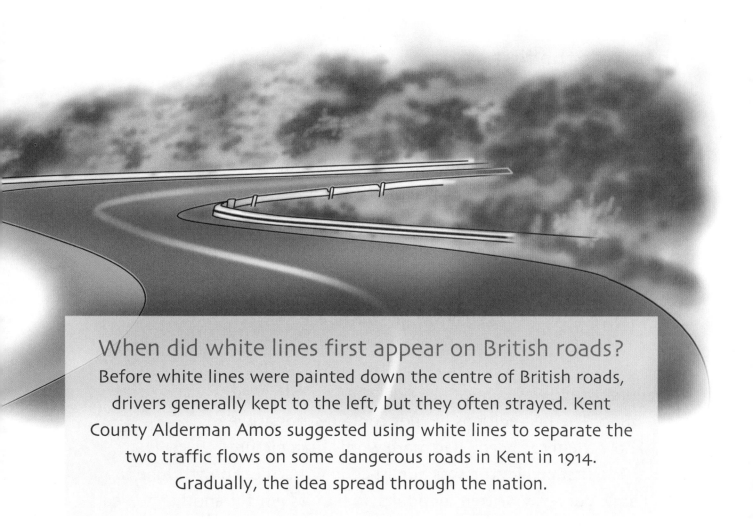

When did white lines first appear on British roads?
Before white lines were painted down the centre of British roads,
drivers generally kept to the left, but they often strayed. Kent
County Alderman Amos suggested using white lines to separate the
two traffic flows on some dangerous roads in Kent in 1914.
Gradually, the idea spread through the nation.

When was the first multistorey car park opened?
The City & Suburban Electric Carriage
Company of London opened their
multi-storey car park in May 1901. It
had seven storeys and a lift to carry
vehicles to the top.

Which country was the first to issue driving licences?
France was the first country to issue
driving licences, in 1893. In the same
year, France also became the first
country to insist upon a driving test for
all motorists.

When were elastic bands first used?
The first elastic bands were
made by Perry and Company of
London in 1845, under a patent
issued to the company on
17th March of that year.

Which was the first newspaper?

Public newspapers as we know them today are a relatively modern development, although attempts to inform the public date back to ancient Rome. Possibly the first 'newspaper' was the acta diurna (daily acts) which were reports of important events designed to inform the people of Rome.

What was the first comic strip in a newspaper?

The first comic strip to appear in a newspaper was The Yellow Kid, which appeared in a colour supplement of The New York Journal on 24th October 1897.

What was the first comic?

The first comic was Comic Cuts, published on 17th May 1890. The first editions did not contain strips as we know them today and had more words than pictures. The first comic strip was published in Comic Cuts on 7th June 1890. Comic Cuts was written for adults and it was not for another 30 years that the first comic for children, The Rainbow, was published.

Who was the first man on the moon?

Neil Armstrong, the American astronaut stepped down from the lunar module 'Eagle' on 20th July 1969, becoming the first human to set foot on the moon.

What were the first words spoken on the moon?

"That's one small step for Man, one giant leap for mankind," uttered Neil Armstrong as he landed on the moon in 1969.

When was a mechanical hare first used in dog racing?

A mechanical hare was first used to entice greyhounds to race in London, on 6th October 1876. The hare was drawn along a straight, 3,645 metre (3,986 yd) track by a rope wound around a windlass. In 1895, a mechanical hare was tried in Ireland but did not prove popular, and it was not until 1923 in the USA that the idea really caught on.

What was the first aeroplane to have a toilet?

The Russian passenger plane Russky Vitiaz, first flown in May 1913, was the first aircraft with a toilet on board.

What was the first railway train to have a toilet?

In 1859, George Pullman installed a toilet at each end of a sleeping car used on the Chicago & Alton railroad.

What was the first credit card?

When people buy things today they often use a credit card. They do not have to pay in cash as the amount of the transaction is charged direct to their bank account or they pay part or all of the outstanding bill at the end of the month. Shortly after the First World War, petrol companies in the USA began to issue such cards which allowed people to get petrol without having to pay for it at the time. After the Second World War, this idea spread to hotels and department stores, which began issuing their own cards. The first credit card to cover all types of purchases was Diners Club, which dates back to the early 1950s.

Precious Stones and Metals

What are the crown jewels?

The crown jewels are a collection of jewellery and regalia that symbolises the authority of the British monarchy. The jewels are sometimes worn by the monarch on state occasions. Among the most important items are the Imperial State Crown, the Royal Sceptre (which holds the largest cut diamond in the world) and the Sword of State.

Who tried to steal the crown jewels?

In 1671, Captain Thomas Blood pretended to fall in love with the jewel-keeper's daughter to get himself into the Tower of London. He pretended to be a clergyman and the jewel keeper believed him. Blood knocked the man on the head and stole some crowns. He did not get very far though, before he was stopped by an off-duty soldier. Much to everyone's surprise the King, Charles II, pardoned Blood and even awarded him a special pension for his daring deed!

Where are the crown jewels kept?

In the Tower of London. In 1994, they were moved to a special display centre, in the former Waterloo Barracks.

What is black diamond?

There are dark diamonds that are, sometimes, called 'black' but the term is more often used to describe coal.

Why are diamonds valuable?

The value of a precious stone or metal is determined by its appearance and rarity. For centuries, diamonds have been regarded as the most brilliant of precious stones, for when cut they are particularly attractive in the way they reflect light. At one time, diamonds were extremely rare and were used more as symbols of power than as jewellery. This was so until the 15th century, when ladies of the royal court of France started a fashion for diamond jewellery. There has been a demand ever since!

What is bronze?

Bronze is an alloy of copper and tin. It is one of the oldest metal alloys known to Man and has been used since about 5000 BC. Bronze is extremely strong and does not rust or corrode.

What is an alloy?

An alloy is a blend of metal with one or more other metals. Most are made by melting one metal and then adding the others. The alloy is usually much harder or stronger than any of the metals used to make it.

What unit is used for weighing gold?

Gold, diamonds and other precious stones are weighed in carats. The name comes from the seeds of the locust bean, which were once used to weigh precious stones.

Who would use a crampon?

A crampon is a type of metal plate with spikes on it. Mountaineers attach crampons to their boots to give them a better grip in snow and ice.

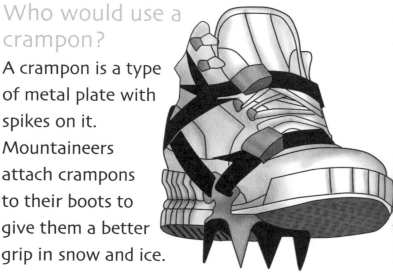

What is Fort Knox?

Fort Knox is the USA's gold depository, situated in Hardin, Kentucky. It contains much of the nation's gold reserves.

Which metal is liquid?

At normal temperature, just one metal is in liquid state - mercury. It has to be at 40°C (120°F) to become a solid.

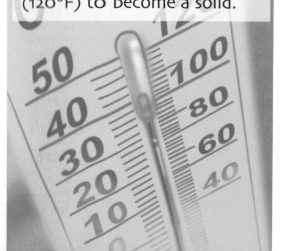

For how much are the crown jewels insured?

Because they are of such great historical significance and immense importance to the country, the crown jewels are not insured. It is estimated that they are worth over £100 million, so great care is taken to ensure that they are very well protected.

How much gold is in Fort Knox?

The actual amount of gold stored in Fort Knox is a closely guarded secret. The depository - a bomb-proof building constructed of concrete, steel and granite and equipped with numerous security devices - is guarded day and night.

Faiths and Beliefs

Who was Buddha?

Gautam of Siddhartha (circa 563-483 BC) was brought up in India, in luxury. When he was 29, he gave up his wealth to seek the true meaning of life. Six years later, he found enlightenment, hence the name Buddha, meaning 'the enlightened one'. He then devoted the rest of his life to teaching others how to find enlightenment and Buddhism is now one of the great world religions.

What is the 'Wailing' Wall?

The Wailing Wall is a sacred place in Jerusalem. It was built in AD 70 on the former site of King Solomon's Temple, which was destroyed by the Romans. Many people believe prayers given at the wall will be answered. They write the prayers on pieces of paper and place them in cracks in the wall.

What are the seven deadly sins?

The seven deadly sins are pride, avarice, envy, lust, sloth, gluttony and anger.

Why do we have eggs at Easter?

Easter occurs at springtime, which is the start of the growing season. Ancient people used eggs as a symbol of new births, so they became associated with spring. The early Christians adopted this idea and for them eggs represented the resurrection of Jesus Christ. It became common practice to paint eggs and give them to family and friends at Easter.

When were chocolate Easter eggs first made?

Chocolate Easter eggs were first made at the end of the 19th century. Today, in the British Isles alone, over 80 million chocolate eggs are bought every year.

Why are Church lecterns in the form of an eagle?

In many churches, the Bible is placed upon a reading stand called a lectern. Very often this is made of carved wood or brass to represent an eagle with outstretched wings. The eagle is a symbol of Jesus Christ's return to life after his death. It has been a religious symbol for a very long time, but lecterns shaped as eagles were unknown before the 13th century.

Why is Mecca important to Muslims?

Mohammed, founder of the Muslim religion, Islam, was born in Mecca around AD 570. It is the Holy city of Islam. Muslims must face towards it when they pray and visit Mecca at least once in their lifetime.

What was the Holy Grail?

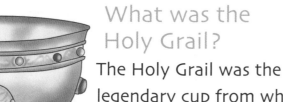

The Holy Grail was the legendary cup from which Jesus drank at the Last Supper. Some tales of King Arthur tell of his knights' search for the Grail.

What is Shinto?

Shinto is an ancient religion of Japan, and the word 'Shinto' means 'The Way of the Gods'. The Gods of Shinto are the forces of nature and, as there were so many of them, it is also known as 'the religion of the million gods'.

What is Halloween?

The word 'Halloween' is an abbreviation of 'All Hallows Evening', the evening before All Saints Day (the word 'hallows' meaning saints). It also has an association with witches, but this goes back to pagan times. The 31st October used to be the last day of the year and was celebrated in the same way that we still celebrate New Year's Eve. It was originally a festival of fire, the dead and the forces of evil. The fire part of the celebrations has now moved to 5th November - Bonfire Night. It was believed that on Halloween the dead rose from the grave and witches roamed the skies on their broomsticks. The ancient celebrations were treated with fear and suspicion, but today Halloween is an occasion to dress up and have fun.

Why are Church lecterns in the form of an eagle ?

In many churches, the Bible is placed upon a reading stand called a lectern. Very often this is made of carved wood or brass to represent an eagle with outstretched wings. The eagle is a symbol of Jesus Christ's return to life after his death. It has been a religious symbol for a very long time, but lecterns shaped as eagles were unknown before the 13th century.

Why is Mecca important to Muslims?

Mohammed, founder of the Muslim religion, Islam, was born in Mecca around AD 570. It is the Holy city of Islam. Muslims must face towards it when they pray and visit Mecca at least once in their lifetime.

What was the Holy Grail?

The Holy Grail was the legendary cup from which Jesus drank at the Last Supper. Some tales of King Arthur tell of his knights' search for the Grail.

What is Shinto?

Shinto is an ancient religion of Japan, and the word 'Shinto' means 'The Way of the Gods'. The Gods of Shinto are the forces of nature and, as there were so many of them, it is also known as 'the religion of the million gods'.

What is Halloween?

The word 'Halloween' is an abbreviation of 'All Hallows Evening', the evening before All Saints Day (the word 'hallows' meaning saints). It also has an association with witches, but this goes back to pagan times. The 31st October used to be the last day of the year and was celebrated in the same way that we still celebrate New Year's Eve. It was originally a festival of fire, the dead and the forces of evil. The fire part of the celebrations has now moved to 5th November - Bonfire Night. It was believed that on Halloween the dead rose from the grave and witches roamed the skies on their broomsticks. The ancient celebrations were treated with fear and suspicion, but today Halloween is an occasion to dress up and have fun.

Food

What is Haggis?

Haggis is a popular Scottish dish made from the finely chopped heart, liver and lungs of a sheep, mixed with onion, oatmeal, herbs and seasoning. These ingredients are put together in the lining of a sheep's stomach and boiled for several hours. The recipe dates back to, at least, the Middle Ages.

What is a bouquet garni?

A bouquet garni is a collection of different herbs (usually tied together) used in cooking. The basic bouquet garni contains a bay leaf and sprigs of thyme and parsley. Marjoram is also a popular herb, while many cooks wrap celery around the herbs before tying them together. Instead of being tied, the herbs can also be placed loosely in a muslin bag. This makes the bouquet easier to find when the cook wants to remove it.

When was tea first brought to Europe?

Tea was introduced to Europe by the East India Company in 1609. Doctors recommended tea as a cure for many ills and some people, reportedly, drank up to 100 cups a day.

Who invented potato crisps?

In 1853, an American Indian chief, George Crum, was working at a hotel in Florida. A customer requested some fried potatoes but wanted them very thinly cut. They were fried, but to a frazzle. Luckily, the customer liked them. Others began asking for the same and the great potato crisp was born.

What is a calorie?

We often hear of calorie-controlled diets, but what exactly is a calorie? It is a unit of heat defined as the amount of energy needed to raise the temperature of a gram of water through one degree centigrade. It is often used to measure the energy value of foods.

How did the chef's hat get its shape?

According to tradition, the chef's hat was originally designed by the great Italian Renaissance painter Leonardo da Vinci (1452-1519). As well as being a painter, sculptor, architect and engineer, he was also a good cook! The hat was then redesigned by Antonin Careme in the late 18th century. In the 19th century, Alexis Soyer starched the pleats so the hat would stay upright and give the chef's head some ventilation.

When were baked beans invented?

Baked beans have been a popular dish since at least the early 19th century. Back then, the making of baked beans in the USA was a weekly affair that involved the whole family. In 1875, the fishermen of Maine wanted to enjoy their beans while away at sea, so a local company, Burnham & Morrill, began canning baked beans.

What is Bombay Duck?

Bombay Duck is a dish of dried, salted fish. The type of fish used is the bummalo, which is rather like salmon. Bombay, India, is one of the main trading centres for this fish - hence 'Bombay' in the name - but where the 'Duck' name comes from is unclear. Bombay Duck is usually eaten as a relish with curries and similar dishes.

When was the pop-up toaster introduced?

The General Electric Company sold the first electric toasters in 1927, in New York. They toasted only one side of the bread, so each slice had to be turned around by hand to toast the other side. The first pop-up toaster, toasting the bread on both sides at once, and releasing the bread after a given time, was invented by Charles Strite of Minnesota.

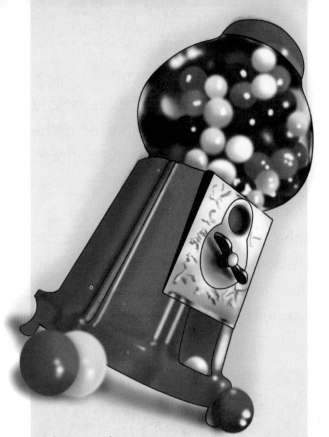

What is Sauerkraut?

Cabbage pickled in brine. Originating from Germany, it is made by packing alternate layers of cabbage and salt in a large barrel. When it has fermented slightly, it is then bottled or canned.

Where does nutmeg come from?

A nutmeg is the hard kernel of an East Indian evergreen. To preserve the flavour, the nutmegs are exported whole and grated only when required to flavour foods.

How is chewing gum made?

A man called a 'chicler' is the first person involved in making chewing gum. It is his job to climb the capodilla tree, where he makes deep gashes in the trunk. The sap, or chicle, leaks from the tree and into a pot on the ground. The chicle is then boiled and poured into moulds to solidify. It is sent to a factory where it is chopped up and boiled again to ensure all the impurities are removed. Vegetable oil is added to soften the chicle, as well as sugar, syrup and flavourings. The blended gum is now formed into a long slab which is cut into sticks before being wrapped.

How did the 'hot dog' get its name?

Near the end of the 19th century, Harry Stevens sold Frankfurter sausages at baseball stadiums in the USA. Because the sausages were hot, he put them in bread rolls. A cartoonist happened to draw Harry's stall but because he could not spell dachshund (Harry's nickname for the sausages), he called them hot dogs - and the name has remained ever since.

What is yoghurt?

Yoghurt is milk which has been impregnated with live bacteria. Plain yoghurt can be eaten as is, or used in a wide variety of cooking. Most yoghurt bought in shops is flavoured with fruit or other foods and is eaten on its own or poured over desserts.

What are raisins?

Raisins are dried grapes which are grown in California, the Mediterranean and Australia. Originally, the grapes were dried in the sun, but now most are dried in specially heated buildings. At one time the word 'raisin' was also used to describe what are now known as currants and sultanas, both of which are also made from dried grapes.

When was wine first made?

The history of wine can be traced back to 1500 BC. It is referred to in the Old Testament of the Bible and the ancient Assyrians and Egyptians were great wine-makers.

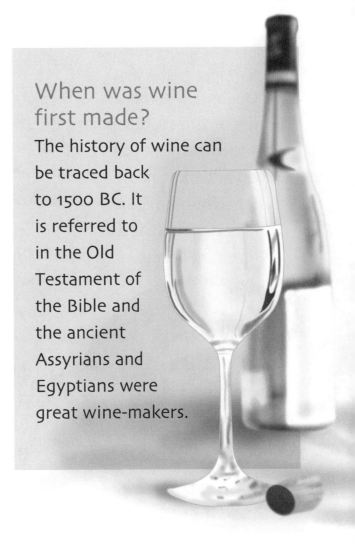

What was the first breakfast cereal?

Henry D Perky, an American, suffered with a bad stomach. One day he saw a man eating whole boiled wheat with milk for breakfast. This seemed the ideal solution to his stomach problems, so in 1893 Perky invented shredded wheat. Two years on, he began producing the cereal on a large scale.

What is tapioca?

Tapioca - delicious when made into a dessert - originates from the poisonous roots of the cassava plant, which grows in tropical regions. When the starchy substance inside the roots is heated, the poison evaporates. The heat also transforms the tapioca into clear pellets, which is how it appears when bought in shops. When cooked in milk, the tapioca softens and swells. In appearance, it resembles frogspawn - the nickname given to it by many British children.

What is caviar?

Caviar is the roe (eggs) of the sturgeon fish to which salt has been added. It has a very strong flavour and is regarded as a great delicacy.

Which country produces the most types of cheese?

There are about 450 named cheeses made around the world. Over half, some 240, are made in France.

Where do hamburgers come from?

Although the hamburger is now associated mainly with the USA, it came originally from Russia. In medieval times, a favourite Russian food was shredded raw meat seasoned with salt, pepper and onion juice. German sailors visiting the Baltic ports, liked the meat and took the recipe back to the port of Hamburg in Germany - hence, the name 'hamburger'. Unable to face the thought of eating the meat raw, the Germans usually grilled it. In the 19th century, German immigrants took the recipe with them to America. In 1900, Louis Larsen served the dish between two slices of bread to make it easier to eat and the American hamburger was born.

What is saffron?

A yellow substance used for colouring and flavouring food. It is made from the stigmas of a particular type of crocus, and is very expensive because it takes over 4,000 stigmas to produce just one ounce.

Why is a chicken wishbone used for wishing?

There are several ancient ways of telling fortunes by using bones. Pulling a wishbone and making a wish has developed from these. It is said that the person who gets the larger part of the wishbone when it is broken will have his or her wish granted.

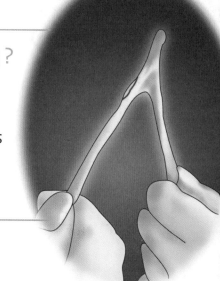

What are Scotch eggs?

Scotch eggs are hard-boiled eggs that have been covered with sausage meat, then coated with breadcrumbs and fried.

What is an ugli?

An ugli is a fruit. It is a cross between a grapefruit, a tangerine and an orange.

What is marzipan?

Marzipan is a paste that is used to cover cakes, or is made into sweets. It is a mixture of sugar and almonds (in fact, it is often called 'almond paste').

Did the Romans eat bread?

Bread was in existence long before Roman times. It has been the staple food of people all over the world. The Romans certainly ate bread and there were almost 260 bakers in Rome alone, around 100 BC. At a later date, the Roman emperor Trajan even founded a school for bakers.

Who invented fish fingers?

The fish finger was invented by the Bird's Eye food company in 1955. By 1994, Bird's Eye had sold some 14 billion!

Where does mace come from?

Mace is a spice widely used in cooking. It is in fact, the outer covering of the nutmeg which has been dried in the sun.

Who put the hole in a ring doughnut?

It is said this innovation was the idea of a boy called Hanson Gregory, in 1847. He enjoyed his mother's doughnuts but they were always doughy in the centre. One day, he suggested she cut out the middle before frying them. The resulting doughnuts were perfect. And so, the ring doughnut was born!

Trees and Plants

Why do trees shed their leaves?

As the days become shorter, the food-making process of leaves slows down and the leaves of deciduous trees wither and fall. This prevents the tree from losing moisture through the leaves' pores, which would be harmful during the winter months.

Where does castor oil come from?

Castor oil is obtained from the seeds of a plant which is sometimes called Palma Christi, but is better known as the castor oil plant. This plant is actually a tall shrub that grows to about 2 metres in height.

How is dew formed?

After a warm day, the temperature drops at night and the air and the water vapour in it become chilled. The water vapour becomes heavy and settles on the cooled leaves of plants.

What do leaves do?

The leaf takes water and minerals absorbed from the soil by the tree's roots, which are carried up to the leaf by tubes. These nutrients combine with carbon dioxide from the air. With the aid of energy from sunlight, it turns these substances into sugar, which is food for the tree.

How did the dandelion get its name?

The name 'dandelion' probably originated in Norman times. People thought the leaves resembled lions' teeth, so the plant was called 'dent de lion' (lion's tooth). Over time 'dent de lion' gradually became 'dandelion'.

Where does cork come from?

Cork is the outer layers of a type of oak tree found in Spain and Portugal.

What is an oak apple?

Oak apples are swellings caused by the gall wasp, which lays its eggs on the oak tree. When the eggs have hatched the grubs eat their way through the spongy flesh of the apple.

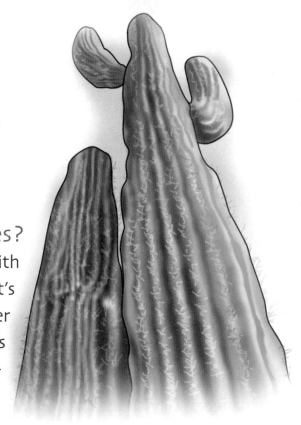

Why do cactus plants have spines?

As the cactus lives in dry regions, it has to cope with lack of water. To absorb water quickly, the plant's roots remain near the surface of the ground; water is stored in its spongy stem. The prickly spines reduce water loss and have one other advantage - a thirsty animal is unlikely to bite into the spiny cactus to quench its thirst!

Where do cashew nuts come from?

Cashew nuts grow on a small evergreen tree found in Central and South America. The shells contain a poisonous substance, which is removed by roasting. Sometimes this poisonous oil is extracted and can be used to protect timber from termites.

What is camomile?

Camomile is a plant, the flowers of which look like daisies. Because it has such a pleasant scent, it was often used in the Middle Ages to spread on the floors of houses to make them smell fresh. When infused with hot water, camomile makes a pleasant drink reputed to ease indigestion and promote relaxation.

How is rubber made?

Rubber is made from latex, a milky fluid obtained from the rubber (Hevea) tree. A groove is cut into the bark and the latex oozes into a cup attached to the tree. The latex is then mixed with an acid, which causes it to coagulate so that it can be pressed into sheet form. It is then crushed and mixed with various chemicals in a process called vulcanisation, which was discovered by Charles Goodyear in 1839. The rubber is then made into the many rubber products that we use today.

Insects

How do grasshoppers hear?

With their stomachs! They do not have ears and rely upon a special hearing organ in their middle section.

Why does a glow-worm glow?

The insects we call glow-worms may be either luminous, wingless beetles or fireflies. On the underside of the glow-worm most familiar in Europe, is a layer of oily tissue that, by chemical action, produces a glow. A second layer of tissue acts as a reflector and the outer transparent skin serves as a lens. Light is produced when the female wishes to attract a mate. With its specially large eyes, the male is able to see the glow and is attracted to it.

What are silverfish?

Silverfish are scaly, wingless insects commonly found in homes, particularly in moist areas or where there is food. They are about 1.7 centimetres (1/2 in) long, covered in silver scales and dart away at great speed when disturbed. They are harmless and, although they eat food scraps, they seldom actually spoil food.

Which food and fabric colouring was made from crushed insects?

The red colouring cochineal was once made from the crushed bodies of a beetle found in Central America. Nowadays it is made from synthetic dyes for clothing and vegetable dyes for food colouring.

How many legs do centipedes and millipedes have?

Centipedes and millipedes are segmented worm-like creatures which have a pair of legs growing from each segment. The word 'centipede' means 'hundred footed' and 'millipede' means 'thousand footed'. Centipedes may have from 28 to over a hundred legs, but millipedes have nowhere near a thousand legs as their name suggests.

How does a fly walk on the ceiling?

Highly magnified pictures of a housefly's foot show that it is composed of two fleshy pads. On these pads are modified hairs which are, in fact, tubes with a mushroom shaped sucker at the ends. From these suckers there is a secretion which is slightly sticky and which enables the fly to stick to any surface. To remove itself from the surface, the fly raises its foot obliquely so that each row of hair is removed separately.

Why is the death's head hawk moth so called?

The death's head hawk moth, found in Europe, acquired its name because the markings on its thorax often look like a human skull.

Where do flies go in winter?

Flies hibernate during the winter months, but many of them die with the onset of cold weather. In order to hatch, the egg of a fly has to be between 24°C (76°F) and 35°C (95°F) - another reason why so few flies are seen in winter.

Do moths eat clothes?

There are six species of moth that damage clothes, carpets and upholstery. But it is not the moth itself that does the damage, it's the moth's larvae. Moths lay eggs on the material and when the larvae hatch they start munching!

How strong is an ant?

An ant is so strong, it can lift fifty times its own weight.

Where does a bee keep its sting?

A bee's sting is at the tip of its abdomen. It consists of a shaft of two barbed lancets running on 'rails' on the pointed stylet. The lancets move forward alternately and penetrate deep into the victim. Poison is then pumped down the central canal and into the wound.

How did the ladybird get its name?

In the Middle Ages this insect was dedicated to the Virgin Mary. It became known as the 'Beetle of Our Lady', which over time was shortened to 'ladybird'.

Are ladybirds useful?

Ladybirds are certainly useful to gardeners because they feed on aphids (tiny insects), which can damage plants. Some market gardeners buy ladybirds for their plants, to control pests without using harmful chemicals.

How many types of ladybirds are there?

There are some 3,000 species of ladybirds around the world.

Are ladybirds known by any other names?

Yes, in the USA the bright beetles are called ladybugs.

What is a ladybird's favourite colour?

Many aphids that ladybirds eat tend to be found on yellow flowers. Wear a yellow T-shirt in summer and you may end up covered with ladybirds!

Why is the deathwatch beetle so called?

This beetle acquired its strange name because people once believed the clicking sound it makes is a sign of impending death. The beetle burrows through wood, and the sound is actually the female beetle tapping its head against the tunnel walls to attract a mate.

Why is the black widow spider so called?

The black widow is a poisonous spider found in North America. It is all black except for a red, hour-glass-shaped mark on its underside. It is called the black widow because the female often eats her mate!

What is the biggest beetle?

The biggest beetle in the world is the goliath beetle, which lives in Africa. It can measure up to 11.4 cm (4.5 in) long and weigh up to 100 grams (3.5 oz).

How strong is spiders' silk?

It is thought the silk spun by spiders to make webs is stronger than steel. At one time the US military were planning to make a bullet-proof jacket made of spiders' silk.

Birds and Animals

How do you determine the age of a tortoise?

A tortoise's shell consists of plates, which are covered with horny shields. On these shields there are rings. The number of rings determines the creature's age in years. This system only works with young tortoises, for as they get older the shields are worn smooth.

Who was killed by a tortoise?

According to comic legend the Greek poet Aeschylus was killed by a tortoise. Aeschylus was bald, and it is said that an eagle mistook his head for a stone. It dropped the tortoise it was carrying, hoping that the 'stone' would break the shell. Unfortunately it killed the poet instead!

How fast can a mole dig?

A mole can dig a tunnel two metres long in just 12 minutes. It is not unusual for a mole to dig a tunnel of 100 metres (329 ft) in length in just one night.

What is an aardvark?

The aardvark is about the size of a pig and has very long ears. It lives in central and southern Africa and its name, from the Boer language, means 'earth pig'.

Why does a hippopotamus live in water?

The water helps to support the immense weight of the hippopotamus. Life could be quite uncomfortable for the animal if it had to live on land. They do, however, come out of the water quite a lot, particularly at night.

What is a duck-billed platypus?

This strange river creature lives in Australia and Tasmania. It has a soft duck-like bill, webbed feet and a broad tail. It is one of only two mammals that lay eggs, the other being the spiny anteater.

What is an echidna?

An echidna is a spiny, egg-laying, burrowing animal that lives in Australia and New Guinea. It is a type of anteater and looks like a hedgehog. When attacked, it rolls itself up into a ball.

Are pigs dirty animals?

No, pigs like to live in clean conditions. They do, however, wallow in mud in hot weather - the mud helps to keep them cool.

Which is the smallest mammal?

Not a great deal is known about the Savi's white-toothed pygmy shrew, which lives in Southern Europe and Africa. It is about 4 centimetres (1.5 in) long, has a tail of 2 centimetres (3/4 in) and weighs around 2 grams (0.07 oz) which makes it the smallest non-flying mammal known to Man.

What is a burro?

It is a small domesticated ass that is used as a pack animal and is found mainly in Mexico.

Which dog does not bark?

The basenji, which comes from Africa, does not bark.

Where would you find a dingo in the wild?

A dingo is the wild dog of Australia. Its origin is uncertain, but some people believe that the Aborigines brought it from Asia.

Why do dogs bury bones?

When dogs lived in the wild, they were always under threat of attack by other dogs while eating. So, they ate as quickly as they could and buried any food left over to save for the future. Burying a meaty bone and leaving it in the earth for a while also softened the meat, making it easier to eat. The domesticated dogs of today have no need to bury, but retain the habit just the same.

How do you determine a horse's age?

By looking at its teeth. When a horse is very young it has only incisors. At the age of four, its milk teeth should have been replaced by permanent teeth. By looking at the growth and shape of the permanent teeth, an expert can estimate the horse's age up to about nine years. At about ten years of age a groove (called Galvayne's groove) appears on the rear incisors. Slowly the groove increases in length, and by the time the horse is 15, it is half the length of the tooth. When the horse is between 25 and 30, Galvayne's groove gradually disappears.

Which is the tallest dog?

The tallest dogs are great danes, which can be up to 81 centimetres (32 in) high at the shoulder. Great danes were originally bred in Germany some 400 years ago, for hunting wild boar.

Which is the smallest breed of dog?

The chihuahua can weigh as little as 0.5 kilograms (1.1 lb). It is named after a Mexican mining town. Other dogs of similar size are the toy poodle and the Yorkshire terrier. In fact, the smallest dog on record was a Yorkshire terrier weighing 113 grams (4 oz).

Why do dogs turn around before lying down?

When dogs were wild, they would turn round and round to trample down the grass to make a comfortable bed upon which to sleep. Even though dogs have now been domesticated for thousands of years and have no need to do this, the habit remains.

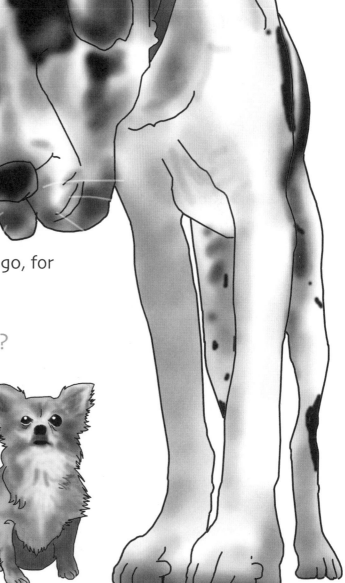

Why do cats scratch furniture?

They do this to exercise their claws. Usually it is only cats which spend a lot of time indoors that do this. Cats that have plenty of freedom outdoors find trees or fences to scratch.

Why do cats always fall on their feet?

When a cat falls, it immediately turns its head to face the ground. Almost instantly the muscles of the body react, turning the rest of the body around so that the whole of the cat is in the correct position - feet first - before it reaches the ground.

Why are tigers striped?

A tiger's stripes act as a form of natural camouflage. One of the largest and most beautiful members of the cat family, the tiger is found mainly in Central and Southern Asia. Much of his area is jungle or grassy plain and the tiger's striped coat blends with the bamboos and slender grass that are found here, making the animal difficult to see. This is an important advantage when the tiger is hunting for prey.

Where can you find a cat without a tail?

The Isle of Man in the Irish Sea is the home of the tail-less Manx cat. Another breed of tail-less cat can be found in Japan and it is believed that the Manx breed originated in the Far East.

Is there anything else unusual about the Manx cat?

Yes. Its rear legs are longer than its front ones, thus giving it a curious hopping motion when it walks.

Why do cats have whiskers?

Cats' whiskers are embedded in a mass of tissue which contains many nerves. This makes the whiskers so sensitive that the cat can use them to measure the width of an opening, or to sense nearby objects when there is not enough light to see clearly.

Which is the fastest animal on earth?

Given level conditions and open ground, the cheetah is the fastest. It can run up to 100 kilometres per hour (62 mph). It can maintain this speed for about 500 metres (547 yds).

What is catgut?

Catgut is a strong cord made from the intestines of sheep and other animals. It is used for stringing certain musical instruments and sports rackets. When sterilized, it is used as surgical thread.

Does catgut come from cats?

No. The 'cat' in 'catgut' is most likely derived from 'cattle' rather than 'cat'. Catgut is made from the intestines of sheep (and occasionally from horses, cattle and pigs).

Why do cats purr?

Although cats seem to purr with pleasure, it is more likely that this noise is made to let others know of the cat's presence. A mother cat, for example, purrs to let her kittens know she is still around.

What is the largest land mammal?

The African elephant. Adult males can weigh up to 8 tons and measure some 3-4 metres (10-13 ft) in height at the shoulder.

Which animal has the longest nose?

The African elephant, whose trunk measures 2.5 metres (8 ft 3 in).

What is the difference between Indian and African elephants?

Although at first sight, the African and Indian elephants look alike, there are quite a few differences between them. For one, the African elephant has bigger ears than its Indian cousin. The head of the African elephant is more rounded and its eyes are larger. There are also differences in the trunks; that of an African elephant appears to be made up of segments and it has two small extensions at its tip, whereas the Indian has only one. The African elephant also has larger tusks, and only three nails on its hind feet, while the Indian elephant has four.

Which animal has the longest tail?

The Indian elephant - it has a tail of 1.5 metres (5 ft), not counting the tuft of hair at its end.

Why are elephants often called Jumbo?

Jumbo was the name given to the first African elephant to appear at London Zoo in 1865. Many elephants since have been given the same name and, because he was an exceptionally big elephant the word 'jumbo' is often used to describe anything that is particularly large.

Why do birds eat grit?

As birds do not have teeth, they need some other means of breaking up their food, to prepare it for digestion. The grit eaten by some birds and the small bones consumed by birds of prey, goes into the gizzard with the food. Here, the muscular walls churn the grit or bones and food together. Softened by this action, the food continues on its way through the rest of their digestive system.

How long is a giraffe's neck?

On average a giraffe's neck measures about 2 metres (6 ft 5 in) long. The giraffe is the tallest land animal and can grow up to 5.5 metres (18 ft).

Why do birds sing a dawn chorus?

A dawn chorus is simply each bird proclaiming its right to its territory. In this way, the bird warns others of the same species not to come too close.

What was the elephant bird?

The elephant bird (so called because of its size) lived in Madagascar in the Indian Ocean. A relative of the ostrich, it stood three metres (ten ft) tall and weighed up to 453 kilograms (1,000 lb). Its egg was 200 times bigger than a hen's egg. Madagascans would drill holes in the eggs and use them as water carriers - which held up to 14 litres (18 pints) of liquid! Sadly, the elephant bird is no longer alive - it became extinct over 300 years ago.

How fast can an ostrich run?

The ostrich is the fastest creature on two legs, so it can run pretty fast! It runs at usual speeds of 50 kilometres per hour (30 mph). But it can reach speeds of up to 70 kilometres per hour (43 mph) when escaping from predators.

Where do budgerigars come from?

A budgerigar is a species of Australian parakeet. The name 'budgerigar' comes from the Australian aborigine language and means 'good cockatoo'. In the wild, budgies are usually pale green with yellowish heads and brown bars on the wings. Breeding in captivity has developed other colours such as blue, white and mauve. The first pair were brought to England in 1840.

Why do woodpeckers peck?

Woodpeckers peck at trees to grab insects on the bark. They also peck to make a noise in the same way that other birds sing. And, of course, they peck to make a hole in a tree in which to build a nest.

Where do bats go in the daytime?

Bats are nocturnal creatures - they come out at night. During the day they sleep, hanging upside down in some quiet dark place, like a barn or a cave.

The name of which animal means 'no drink'?

In the language of the Australian aborigine, 'koala' means 'no drink'. It is an appropriate name as the koala seldom needs to drink water - it gets all the water it needs from eating eucalyptus leaves.

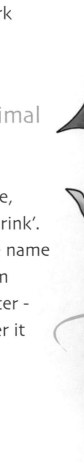

Reptiles

Which is the longest snake?

The Asiatic reticulated python is the longest snake in the world. It lives in southeast Asia and is over eight metres (26 ft) in length.

What is a gecko?

The gecko is a small insect-eating lizard. It has a large head and a short, stocky body. Geckos are quite common in warm countries and they get their strange name from the clicking sound they make.

How strong is an alligator's jaw?

An alligator's jaw is actually quite weak. A man could easily hold an alligator's mouth shut - but it is not to be recommended!

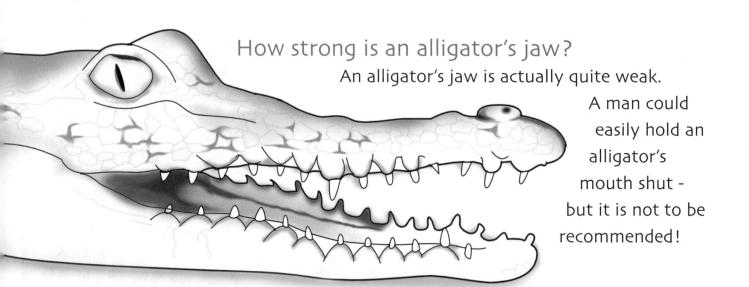

Why do snakes stare?

Snakes appear to be staring simply because they do not have eyelids to cover their eyes as we do. This means that even when resting or hibernating, the snake's eyes are always open. Instead of eyelids snakes have a transparent membrane over the eyes to protect them.

Are lizards poisonous?

Yes, but only two species: the gila monster and the Mexican bearded lizard. They are found in parts of Mexico and the USA.

Is it true that lizards squirt blood from their eyes?

Some members of the horned lizard family do squirt blood from their eyes as an unusual means of defence. The blood is thought to cause an irritation to the eyes of any enemy who gets too close.

How does a rattlesnake rattle?

The rattle sound is produced by a number of hollow rings fixed to the end of the snake's tail. The rings are made of a substance similar to that of our finger nails. They are joined loosely and rattle when the snake shakes its tail.

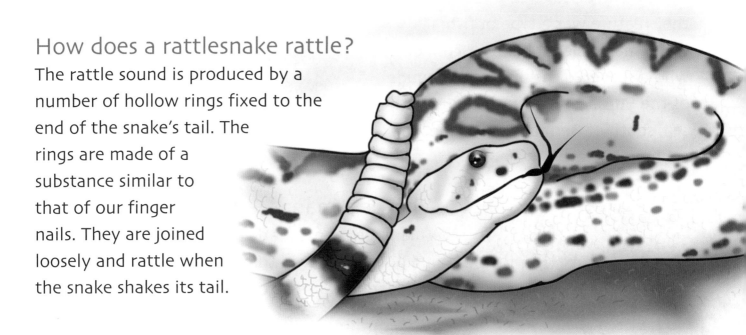

Life Underwater

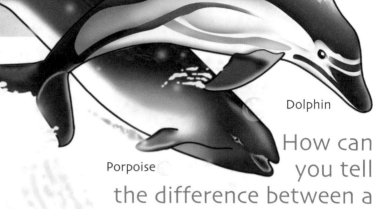

What are plankton?

Plankton are tiny life-forms that float in the sea in groups. The creatures are so small they are invisible to the naked eye, but they are a valuable and essential source of food for whales and other sea creatures.

Porpoise

Dolphin

How can you tell the difference between a dolphin and a porpoise?

The easiest way to tell the difference is to look at the head. Dolphins appear to have a beak, whereas the head of a porpoise is rounded.

How is coral formed?

Coral is made up of the skeletons of small creatures that live in the sea. The corals tend to live in large colonies, which build up over time to form coral reefs.

Where do eels come from?

This question puzzled biologists for centuries. An eel larva was first found in 1856 but Mondini, the Italian who discovered it, believed the creature was a type of fish. It was a man called Johannes Schmidt who discovered the breeding grounds of the European eel, in the Sargasso sea, south of Bermuda. The American eel breeds nearby.

What is a piranha?

The piranha is a fish that lives in the rivers of South America. It is part-icularly famous for its voraciousness. Four of the dozen or so species of piranha fish are dangerous. Pygocentrus piraya - the largest species - can reach lengths of up to 60 centimetres (2ft).

What is a manatee?

A manatee is an aquatic mammal of the sea-cow family. It is believed that these creatures inspired the legendary stories of mermaids.

Who was Pelorus Jack?

Pelorus Jack was the name of a porpoise which, from 1871 to 1912, guided ships through an area of dangerous sea near New Zealand. The waters had many dangerous currents and hidden rocks, but by following Jack the ships were able to navigate the channel safely. The porpoise was called Pelorus Jack as the ships sailed from Pelorus Sound.

How do fish breathe?

First, the fish takes water into its mouth. The water is forced over the gills inside the fish and out through the gill slits, which are usually on each side of the back part of the head. Blood vessels in the gills extract oxygen from the water and the blood then carries it around the body.

What is a seahorse?

Although it does not look like one, the seahorse is actually a fish. There are several different species of seahorse, found in warm seas in many parts of the world. They range in length from two centimetres (3/4 in) to 30 centimetres (11 3/4 in). Seahorses live among seaweed, hanging onto it with their tails. And as they are a similar colour to seaweed, seahorses are well camouflaged there.

Which is the biggest fish?

The whale shark. It lives in the warm parts of the Atlantic, Pacific and Indian Oceans and can measure up to 18 metres (59 ft) long and weigh 20,000 kg (44,092 lb).

Books

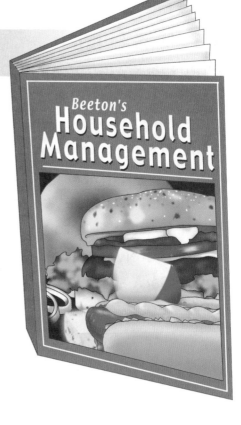

Who was Mrs Beeton?

Isabella Mayson was born in London in 1836. She married Samuel Beeton, a publisher, in 1856. Four years later she wrote her famous cookery book, Household Management.

What is the most famous cookery book?

It has to be Household Management by Isabella Beeton. Although first published in 1861, it contains numerous tips and recipes that are still used today.

Who published the first dictionary?

The first known dictionary was published in 1502. It was produced in Italy by Ambrogio Calepino.

Which was the first printed book?

The earliest mechanically printed book is almost certainly the Gutenberg Bible, which was printed by Johann Gutenberg around 1455.

Which is the world's oldest book?

Although several texts survive from before the birth of Christ, the earliest compiled book is probably the 'Codex Vaticanus' Bible, written in Greek around AD 350. It is preserved in the Vatican Museum, Rome.

Why are maps drawn with north at the top?

Strictly speaking it doesn't matter which way up a map is drawn, provided the directions are indicated. Over many years, however, it has become standard practice to draw maps with north at the top. This convention probably dates back to about AD 160 when the Egyptian astronomer and scientist Claudius Ptolemy drew maps of the then known world. He placed north at the top and map-makers have followed suit ever since.

What is Burke's Peerage?

In 1826, John Burke published the first edition of a book listing all the nobles in Britain. Published every year since, it is entitled Genealogical and Heraldic History of the Peerage, Baronetage, and Knightage of the United Kingdom; it is popularly known as Burke's Peerage.

Who compiled the first encyclopedia?

In AD 77 the Roman scholar Pliny the Elder published the first known encyclopedia, Historia naturalis. It had 2,493 entries, for Pliny tried to cover all known knowledge.

Who would use the Dewey Decimal System?

A librarian or someone using a library are the people most likely to use the Dewey Decimal System. The system is a method of classifying books so they can be easily sorted and found on the shelves. The main part of the system breaks down all knowledge into ten subject areas. Each area is then broken down further into ten sub-classes, which are broken down yet again into ten more sub-classes. Although it has been modified since its creation by Melvil Dewey in 1876, the Dewey System is still used in libraries today.

Who were the Brontë sisters?

Charlotte, Emily and Anne Brontë were all 19th-century novelists. With their mother dead and their father a recluse, they would write stories together to pass the time. Eventually their ability to create fantasy was rewarded in the publication of their books, which today are among the classics of literature.

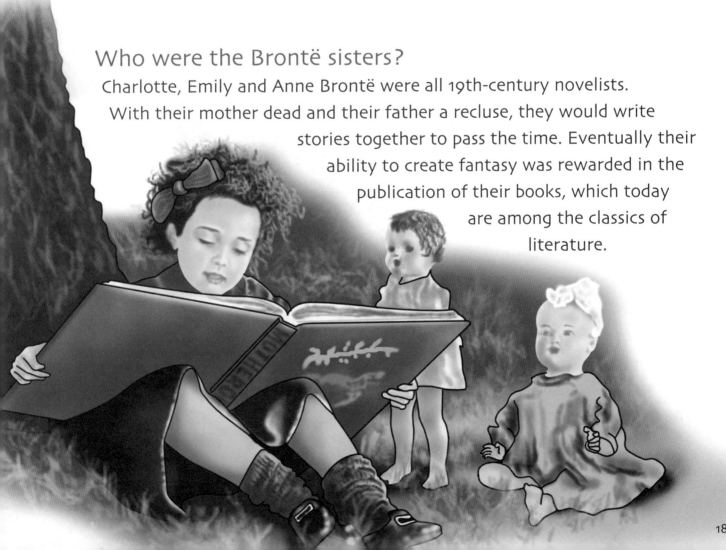

Making Music

How does one play an aeolian harp?

The aeolian harp is an oblong box over which strings of different thicknesses are stretched. It is a musical instrument, yet no-one plays it. To use an aeloian harp, it must be placed outside, where the wind can blow on it. The wind makes the strings vibrate to produce musical sounds. It gets its name from Aeolus, the Greek god of the winds.

What is a Stradivarius?

It is a violin. For almost 200 years the Amati family of Cremona, Italy, made superb violins. One of the family's apprentices was Antonio Stradivarius. Stradivarius violins were beautifully made and gave an excellent tone. As a result, they have become extremely valuable. Stradivarius is now regarded as the greatest violin maker of all time.

What is a Cor Anglais?

Cor Anglais is another name for the English horn, which is a reed instrument of the oboe family.

What is a concerto?

A concerto is a piece of music composed for a solo instrument, accompanied by an orchestra. The purpose of a concerto is to highlight the expertise of the soloist.

Who wrote the most concertos?

Antonio Vivaldi, who composed almost 500 known concertos (though some experts believe he wrote many more). Vivaldi also holds the record for the concerto with the most soloists. He wrote two concertos in which there are 11 soloist parts.

Vibraphone

Tuba

Piano

Strings

First Violins

Viola

Who invented the clarinet?

The clarinet is a single-reed woodwind instrument. It was invented in its current form in about 1700, by Johann Christoph Denner. It has been popular with orchestras and jazz musicians since 1920.

Who invented the saxophone?

The saxophone was invented around 1840 by the Belgian craftsman Adolphe Sax. It was first played publicly in 1844 in Paris, where Sax had a workshop. It is said the instrument was held together with string and sealing wax.

What is a plectrum?

If you watch guitarists, you will see they are often plucking the strings with a plectrum - a small piece of bone or plastic. Plectrums prevent the fingers from becoming sore.

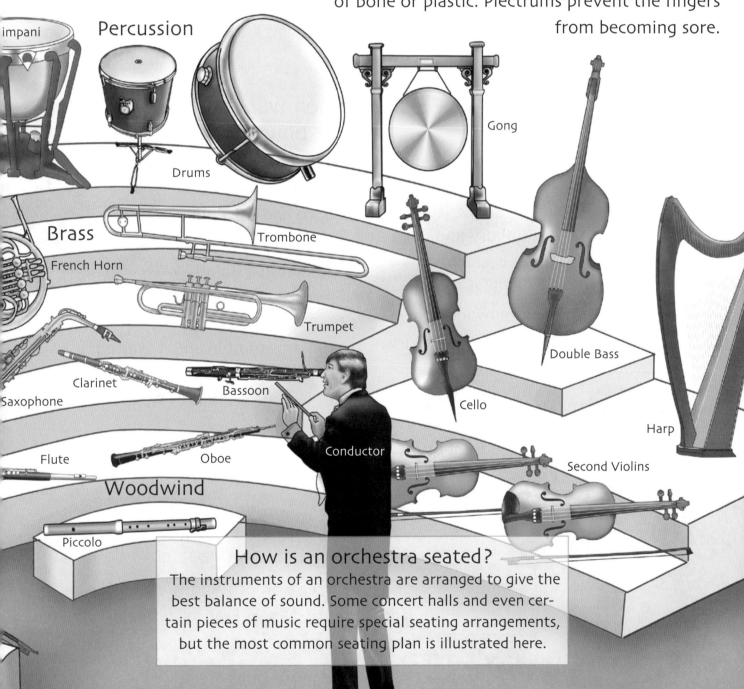

impani

Percussion

Drums

Gong

Brass

Trombone

French Horn

Trumpet

Double Bass

Clarinet

Bassoon

Saxophone

Cello

Harp

Flute

Oboe

Conductor

Second Violins

Woodwind

Piccolo

How is an orchestra seated?

The instruments of an orchestra are arranged to give the best balance of sound. Some concert halls and even certain pieces of music require special seating arrangements, but the most common seating plan is illustrated here.

Games and Sports

Who was the first person to swim the English Channel?

Matthew Webb entered the water at Dover at 12.56 pm on 24th May 1875. Next day, he stepped ashore at Cap Gris-Nez, France, becoming the first person to swim the English Channel without a life jacket. It took him 21 hours 45 minutes and it is thought that he actually swam a distance of 61 kilometres (38 miles) to make the 33 km (21 miles) crossing because tides pushed him off course.

How did the Derby get its name?

In 1779, Sir Charles Bunbury and Lord Derby tossed a coin to decide the name of a race to be held at Epsom for the first time the following year. If it hadn't been for the fact that Lord Derby won the toss, the race could now be known as the Bunbury.

How old is chess?

Chess is an ancient game. The name 'chess' comes from the Persian word 'shah' (meaning king or ruler) and old Persian and Indian writings show the game was known in these countries as early as the 6th century.

When was football first played?

Ball games similar to football can be traced back to ancient China, Greece and Rome, but the origins of the modern game stem from England. The original game was a disorganised rough-and-tumble and it was not until 1846 that the first deliberate rules were formulated. The modern game, however, was formally established with the formation of the Football Association in 1863.

Who was the first woman to swim the English Channel?

Gertrude Ederle on 6th August 1926. She swam from Cap Gris-Nez in France to Deal in England in 14 hours 39 minutes.

When was the first Oxford-Cambridge boat race?

The boat race between Oxford University and Cambridge University is an annual event that attracts the interest of people all over Britain. The first race took place in 1829 at Henley-on-Thames.

How did the Oaks horse race get its name?

The Oaks, run annually at Epsom, received its name from Lambert's Oaks, a cluster of trees near the racecourse. The race was first run in 1779.

When were jigsaw puzzles invented?

John Spilsbury, a teacher at Harrow school in the 1760s, was searching for a new way to teach his pupils geography. One day he cut up a map of the British Isles and asked his class to reassemble it. The idea proved successful, and soon 'dissected puzzles' (as they were then called) became a fashionable tool for teaching geography, history and religion. These first puzzles did not interlock, and were produced for educational purposes only. Interlocking puzzles were developed in the 20th century.

Who invented snooker?

Credit for the game's invention is given to a British Army colonel, Sir Neville Chamberlain, who in 1875 first played the game at his club in India.

How was rugby invented?

During a football match at Rugby School in 1823, a pupil, William Webb Ellis, picked up the ball and ran with it. The idea caught on and the game was soon played at other schools. The Rugby Football Union was founded on January 26th 1871.

What is the Calcutta Cup?

It is an award given to the winner of the annual Rugby Union game between England and Scotland. It is so called because the cup was made from rupees left in the bank by the Calcutta Rugby Club (which was disbanded in 1878).

When was overarm bowling first used in cricket?

In the early days of cricket, it was the custom for bowlers to bowl underarm. Now overarm bowling is the norm. The person responsible for this change was John Willes of Kent, but it seems that the real credit should go to his sister, Christine. Christine used to bowl for John at their home to give him batting practice, but the fullness of her skirt made it impossible for her to bowl underarm. John found the round-arm style she developed more difficult to parry. He adopted the same style but umpires accused him of throwing. In spite of frequent 'no ball' decisions and spectators rushing onto pitches in protest, he persevered with his new delivery. But in 1822, when Kent played the MCC at Lords, a 'no ball' call proved just too much. Willes stormed off the field, mounted his horse, and rode out of the cricket ground for good. Thirteen years later the rules were changed and overarm bowling received official blessing.

How wide is a cricket bat?

In 1776, Mr White of Surrey played cricket with a bat so large it obscured the wicket. Two days later the Hambledon Club, then the ruling body of English cricket, decreed that cricket bats be no more than 10.8 centimetres (4.25 in) wide, a rule that still applies today.

Was cricket ever banned?

Yes, during the reign of Henry VIII. Anyone caught playing cricket on the King's land was fined £20 and sent to prison for up to three years.

Has anyone ever scored 6 runs off 6 balls in cricket?

Sir Garfield Sobers achieved this amazing feat at Swansea in 1968. The ball with which he made this record score is now on display in the museum at Nottingham cricket ground.

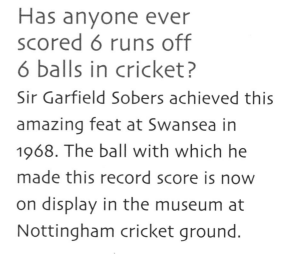

Who invented the crossword puzzle?

It was Arthur Wynne in 1913. A newspaper editor, he was searching for something 'fun' for his paper New York World. The first crossword puzzle was published on 21 December and became an instant success.

What has been the most unusual reason for stopping a cricket match?

One of the most unusual reasons must have been during a match in South Africa: there was an urgent telephone call for one of the players - his wife wanted to know where he had put the soap!

Who invented Monopoly?

Charles Darrow, a heating engineer of Philadelphia, USA, devised the game of Monopoly between 1931 and 1933. He offered it to the USA's foremost games manufacturer, but they turned it down because it was too complicated. Darrow then decided to print some boards himself. The game became quite popular and Parker Brothers changed their mind. They first sold it nationally at Christmas 1935 and it remains popular all over the world to this day.

Which horse race was named after a Tsar?

The Cesarewitch, first run in 1839, was named after the Tsarevitch (or Cesarewitch) Alexander, later Alexander II, who was in England at the time.

When was the Grand National first run?

The Grand National was first run in 1837. This famous steeplechase covers a distance of some seven kilometres (four miles) and is held annually at Liverpool's Aintree Racecourse.

What is the Calgary Stampede?

This is an annual rodeo (a sort of tournament for cowboys) held in Calgary, Canada.

What is a boomerang?

It is a curved, flat piece of wood best known as a weapon of the Australian aborigine. There are two types of boomerangs, the war boomerang (which does not return to the thrower) and the sporting boomerang (which does come back if it has not hit anything). Sporting boomerangs can be anything up to half a metre in length but the war boomerang is twice as long and usually requires both hands to throw it.

Which swords are used in the sport of fencing?

There are three weapons used in modern fencing: the foil, the épée and the sabre.
The foil has a long thin blade with a button on its tip, the épée is stiffer and heavier than the foil and the sabre has a flat blade.

Where was the first ever World Cup held?

Uruguay in 1930. Uruguay beat Argentina 4-2.

What is the Ryder Cup?

Every two years, professional male golfers from Britain and Ireland play a team from the USA. The winning team is given the Ryder Cup, which was first awarded by Samuel Ryder in 1927.

Has anyone ever disputed a cricket umpire's decision?

This happens on occasion, but the most dramatic case occurred during a match between teams from Kent and Essex in 1776. The match ended in a gunfight and three players were shot dead!

Why do some trousers have turn-ups?

King Edward VII was one of the first men to wear turn-ups. It's not known who invented the style but according to tradition, there is a story of an Englishman who was invited to a party in New York. He turned up his trouser legs because it was raining. When he arrived at the party everyone thought this was a new English fashion and the idea caught on.

What is a kimono?

A traditional Japanese costume consisting of a single piece of silk which is held around the waist by a sash.

What is batik?

Batik is an Indonesian technique of dying fabric. Wax is applied to areas that are not to be dyed and then the material is placed in a cool dye. To remove the wax, the material is then set in hot water. This action can be repeated several times with different colours and patterns.

What is Morse Code?

Morse code is a method of sending messages by a series of long and short signals. The signals are sent using a telegraph or by flashes with a torch. In written form, dots represent short signals, dashes long ones.

Where is the Bermuda Triangle?

The Bermuda Triangle covers a vast area of the Atlantic Ocean between Bermuda, Puerto Rico and Miami. Many strange stories have been told of the mysterious disappearances of ships and aeroplanes in this area. But similar tales are told of other parts of the world, and usually improve with each telling. It is impossible to say for certain how much of the Bermuda Triangle mystery is fact and how much is fiction.

NORTH AMERICA
BERMUDA
BERMUDA ISLAND

WEST INDIES

Straits

JAMAICA
Caribbean Sea

Did Sir Walter Raleigh lay down his cloak for the Queen?

According to tradition, Raleigh laid his cloak over a puddle so that Queen Elizabeth I could walk on it and not get her feet wet. Although a nice story, it is an unlikely one. It was probably made up by the British historian Thomas Fuller, who liked to put interesting tales in his writing to pep up any dull parts!

When was tartan banned?

It was against the law to wear tartan dress in Scotland following the Scottish Rebellion of 1745. The ban remained in force until the law was abolished in 1782.

Why is there a best man at weddings?

Being best man at a wedding is an honour few men would welcome, if they realised what they're supposed to be best at. The answer is fighting! In days gone by it was the best man's job to defend the bride and groom should anyone try to take the girl away. The best man had to do the fighting because the groom had other matters on his mind!

What is the Blarney Stone?

It is a stone high up in the battlements of Blarney Castle in Ireland. Kissing the stone is said to give one eloquence. But the stone is on the outside wall and one has to lean over with someone holding onto one's legs to reach it!

What happened to Sir Walter Raleigh's head after his execution?

Legend has it that after Raleigh's execution in 1618, his wife kept his head. She carried it around with her in a bag for 29 years, until her own death.

How is glass produced?

The three basic ingredients are mixed with cullet (broken glass), dolomite and saltcake and are then melted down in a furnace. The intense heat causes the substances to fuse into one molten mass, which flows out of the furnace into a float chamber. Here, the glass floats on a bed of molten tin. The glass is cooled slightly and then passed over water-cooled pipes. Further cooling is achieved by passing the glass under a series of water sprays which also helps to strengthen it. When the glass has cooled completely, it is cut to size.

What is glass made of?

Glass is made by fusing sand with soda ash and lime or with lead oxide. It is thought the ancient Egyptians were the first people to make glass.

What is topiary?

Topiary is the art of clipping hedges and bushes into ornamental shapes. A new plant is usually trained to grow around a wire shape and is clipped regularly to maintain that shape.

Is it possible to be afraid of a messy room?

Yes, a person who has an irrational fear of untidiness is said to be suffering from ataxiophobia.

Is the Willow Pattern Chinese?

No, the pattern was designed by an English potter, Thomas Turner, in about 1780. After it became popular in England, the pattern was copied by Chinese potters to sell their wares to the British.

Is there a story in the Willow Pattern?

The Willow Pattern is said to tell the story of a Chinese girl who ran off with her father's secretary. The father pursued the couple but they were then transformed into doves so they could escape him.

Why are typewriter keys arranged in a certain order?

At first sight, it would appear that a typewriter keyboard is laid out in a nonsensical way. The top line of keys, for instance, are QWERTYUIOP. There is a reason for this odd arrangement. When Christopher Latham Sholes and his colleagues invented the first practical typewriter in 1873, they had quite a problem with the typebars clashing together.

To overcome this, they arranged the keys so that the most used letters in the English language were positioned well apart. This design proved so successful that much the same layout is used to this day.

What is an arctophile?

Someone who collects teddy bears!

Who invented the typewriter?

Henry Mills, an English engineer, was awarded a patent in 1714 for a machine that impressed letters on paper. Over the next 150 years, many other writing machines were invented, some more successful than others, but it was not until 1873 that the forerunner of the modern typewriter was introduced. Christopher Latham Sholes, Carlos Glidden and Samuel Soule persuaded the Remington company to produce their design, which came onto the market a year later.

What was the earliest form of shorthand?

A system created by Marcus Tiro in 63 BC. He used his shorthand to record the speeches of Cicero, a Roman statesman.

What is touch-typing?

Touch-typing is the skill of using a typewriter without looking at the keys. The touch-typist uses all the fingers of both hands in the most efficient manner possible.

What was a press gang?

For centuries, the threat of brutal, enforced military service hung over able-bodied men between the ages of 18 and 25. The service was known as impressment, and the bands of ruffians who carried out the recruitment were called press gangs. They would snatch unwary men and condemn them to service under the then harsh conditions of naval ships.

What is a cockney?

Sometimes, the word 'cockney' is used to describe any person from London. This, however, is not correct. To be a true cockney, the person has to be born within the sound of Bow Bells (the bells of the church of St Mary-Le-Bow in Cheapside). The term 'cockney' is also used to describe the speech and accent of people born in this area.

Who was Uncle Sam?

The name 'Uncle Sam' is often used as a nickname for the USA. The term first came into use in New York around 1812. It is said that a butcher, Samuel Wilson, known as Uncle Sam, supplied beef to the US Army. As the meat crates had US (for United States) stamped on them, the meat became known as Uncle Sam's meat. It was not long before the name Uncle Sam was used for the USA itself.

What is the indian 'rope trick'?

It is a magic trick in which a long rope is made rigid and a boy climbs up it to the top. When he reaches the top, he disappears. Magicians, however, believe it is merely a traveller's tale.

Who was killed by a frozen chicken?

During a stagecoach journey, Francis Bacon had the idea that ice and snow could be used to preserve food. He asked the driver to stop, and stuffed a chicken with snow. Unfortunately, Bacon also caught a chill, which resulted in his death.

Who was preserved in brandy?

When Admiral Nelson died at sea in 1805, the doctor had the problem of preserving the body so it could be returned to England for a hero's funeral. He decided that the best thing was to put it in a barrel of brandy.

What is the registration number of the Queen's car?

There is no registration number on the Queen's car. Her Majesty's cars are the only ones in Britain that do not require registration plates.

What is the Lutine Bell?

The Lutine Bell came from the wreck of HMS Lutine, which sank during a storm off the Dutch coast in 1799. The bell was recovered in 1859 and now hangs in the insurance house Lloyds of London. It is rung when important news is to be announced - one ring means good news and two rings means bad news.

Who owns Ayers rock?

The Australian government transferred ownership of Ayers Rock to the Aboriginal people in 1985. The Australian Aborigines regard Ayers Rock as a sacred place and there are many ancient rock paintings in the numerous caves around its base. The enormous rock is incorporated in the Uluru National Park, Central Australia.

How many words are there in the English language?

There are over 600,000 words in the English language, but even the most clever people only know about 20,000. On average, some 2,000 words are used in everyday speech.

What is the world's most widely spoken language?

Mandarin Chinese. The second most widely spoken language is English.

Who composed the song 'Happy Birthday'?

In 1892, Patty Smith Hill and Mildred Hill wrote the song 'Good Morning to You' for pupils at their school in Louisville, Kentucky, USA. Although their tune is now sung with the words 'Happy Birthday to You', this version has been popular only since its publication in 1935. It has been sung all over the world since, and even in space - on 8th March 1969 it was sung by the Apollo IX astronauts.

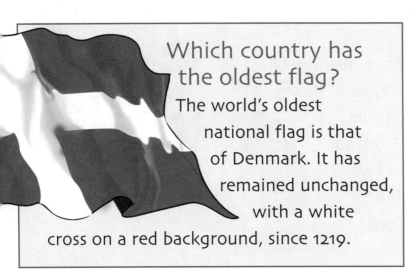

Which country has the oldest flag?

The world's oldest national flag is that of Denmark. It has remained unchanged, with a white cross on a red background, since 1219.

Which British king was crowned on Christmas Day?

William of Normandy, better known as William the Conqueror, in 1066.

How old is the Bank of England?

In 1694, Scottish financier William Paterson suggested a 'Bank of England' be set up in order to lend £1,200,000 to the government. King William III approved the idea on 27th July 1694. It was planned that the bank would close down after a decade, but the Bank of England is now over 300 years old.

Which member of the British royal family was born on Christmas Day?

HRH Princess Alexandra was born on 25th December 1936.

What is the Old Lady of Threadneedle Street?

The Old Lady of Threadneedle Street is a nickname for the Bank of England in Threadneedle Street, London. In 1797, the artist James Gillray depicted the bank as an elderly lady wearing a dress of £1 notes, seated on a chest marked 'Bank of England'.

What was the King's evil?

It was the nickname given to a disease called scrofula. Many believed it could be cured by a touch from the sovereign.

How is lead put into a pencil?

The first stage in the manufacture of pencils consists of making a wooden slat - a flat piece of wood. Several parallel grooves are then cut into each slat. It is into these grooves that the leads (strips of soft graphite) are laid. A second grooved slat is then placed on top of the first, and the two are glued together with the leads in between. The slats are moulded into the shape of pencils before the individual pencils are separated and passed on to the finishing process.

What is the Stone of Scone?

The Stone of Scone is a large piece of sandstone kept at Westminster Abbey in London. It was used in the coronation ceremony for Scottish kings until 1296, when King Edward I took it to England as a war trophy. In 1328, it was agreed that the stone should be returned to Scotland - an agreement that has yet to be fulfilled.

Who stole the Stone of Scone?

Amazingly, the 204 kilogram (450 lb) stone was once stolen from Westminster Abbey! On Christmas Day 1950, four students removed the stone. Months later, it was found at the ruined Abbey of Arbroath, Scotland and police returned it to London. Outside a hotel in Scotland is a replica of the stone but some people believe this is the original and that the one now in Westminster Abbey is the replica!

Does Timbuktu really exist?

Yes, it is a town in West Africa. For many years, it was an important market town and a centre for caravan routes.

Why are clowns often called Joey?

Clowns are often called Joey in honour of Joseph Grimaldi, who lived from 1779 to 1837. Grimaldi was a brilliant clown, singer, dancer and actor and is regarded as one of the greatest clowns of all time.

Why are waste pipes U-shaped?

Waste pipes from toilets and sinks are shaped like a letter U or a letter S to trap water in them. This acts as a seal that prevents foul air from the drains getting into the house.

Why is the piggy bank so called?

Although many piggy banks are shaped like pigs, this is not the reason for their name. The name comes from a ceramic material called 'pygg', which was once used for making ornaments. As the coin saver was made from pygg, it seemed obvious to make it in the shape of a pig.

How old is Buckingham Palace?

Buckingham Palace has been the London residence of British royalty since 1830. The present building stands on the site of Buckingham House, which was built in 1703 for the Duke of Buckingham. King George III bought it for his wife, Queen Charlotte, in 1762 and for the next 50 years it was known as the Queen's House. Work began on the present building in 1825.

Why do we use & for 'and'?

The symbol & (an ampersand) comes from the Latin word 'et' (which means 'and'). The ampersand is simply the 'e' and 't' of et put together. Ampersands are used in hundreds of languages around the world.

What is the Magic Circle?

The Magic Circle is a club for magicians. There are lots of magic clubs around the world where magicians meet to discuss the latest tricks, but the Magic Circle in London is the most famous.

Who put up the famous Hollywood sign?

In 1923, M H Sherman was selling homes in Los Angeles. To publicise the houses, he had a large billboard erected on Lee Mountain with the name of the estate, HOLLYWOODLAND. In 1944, the estate company moved from the area and passed 182 hectares (450 acres) of land, including the sign, to the Los Angeles Parks Department. Five years later, it was rebuilt but the 'land' was removed from it. In 1973, a new sign was built, and was unveiled on 14th November 1978.